How We Christians can Change Ourselves and the World

By

Isaac Oppong-Kyekyeku

Blue Ocean Publishing

The author and the publisher have taken all reasonable care to ensure that all material in this work is original, or is in the Public Domain, or is used with the permission of the original copyright owners. However, if any person believes that material for which they own the copyright has found its way into this work without permission, they should contact the author, via the publisher, who will seek to investigate and remedy any inadvertent infringement.

How We Christians can Change Ourselves and the World
© Isaac Oppong-Kyekyeku 2018

The right of Isaac Oppong-Kyekyeku to be identifed as the author of this work has been asserted by him in accordance with the Copyright, Designs and Patents Act 1988.

All rights reserved. No part of this publication may be reproduced, stored in a retrieval system or transmitted in any form or by any means, electronic, mechanical, photocopying, recording, scanning, or otherwise, without prior written permission of the copyright holder.

Published by Blue Ocean Publishing

www.blueoceanpublishing.biz

A catalogue record for this book is available from the British Library.

ISBN 978-1-907527-37-1

First published in the United Kingdom in 2018 by Blue Ocean Publishing.

Contents

Dedication

This book is lovingly dedicated to all the co-labourers who have so faithfully laboured with my wife and me in the Ministry of God through the UPG Ministry, London; the Ghana Presbyterian Ministry, London; the Elim Pentecostal Church, Coventry and the Grange Park United Reformed Ministry, Leyton, London.

How We Christians can Change Ourselves and the World is already printed in English. The remaining missionary translations and printings are pending.

Acknowledgements

I thank Almighty God for giving me the wisdom and knowledge to write this book.

My thanks also go to the Founder of UPG Ministries Rev. S. K. Boafo, Rev. Dr. E. K. Browne, Word of Life Bible College Principal, Pastor Shadrach Ofosuware, Rev. Samuel Aboagye-Asamoah and Rev. Peter Avery who taught me the 'Word of Life' when I was in the Bible College.

I would also like to thank Alison Oakes, England, for her inspiration and her time to help write and produce this book.

I will always appreciate what you all have imparted to my life. May the Almighty bless all of you.

Aim

The aim of *How We Christians can Change Ourselves and the World* is to let us Christians know our mission: to help God's children refrain from wrongdoing and to change for the better, in order to experience the manifestation of God's presence and power.

It provides an insight into the Word of God and helps the children of God understand that it is time to change and seek God, to enable us to see His glory.

The text of this book assists readers in every situation, and shows how the religion of Jesus Christ allows us to live our lives with great delight. It also shows and assures believers in Christ not to give in to self and Satan, but to let us have the life of Christ and to influence the public.

1 How We Christians can Change Ourselves and the World

Introduction

Who are *Christians* and how can we change ourselves, and the world?

We Christians have repented of our sins and have turned from them, with the desire to make restoration by living new lives, which is the life of God through baptism. We are the people who have agreed to be disciples of Jesus Christ; this indicates that we do whatever Jesus Christ tells us, because we believe that Jesus Christ has paid the price for us and redeemed us from our sins.

We Christians believe that it is only in doing the will of God that we can use the wisdom and knowledge that God has given to us. The Holy Spirit can control us, in order to have an impact on the lives of those people who are in the world.

World

The world refers to all things created by God. It sometimes refers to those people who are doing things that are contrary to the Word of God (Bible).

The world sometimes refers to darkness, meaning that the people in the world are in a dark life, since they do whatever they wish. The darkness includes sin and social injustices, which we experience in life. The people in the world are those people who disregard God's Word and are following their own will or teachings. The world here may also apply to both non-Christians and Christians. Some Christians are also doing the same things as non-Christians, contrary to the Word of God. In some ways, there are no differences between our life and the life of non-Christians.

How We Christians can Change Ourselves and the World

How We Christians can Change Ourselves and the World is concerned with the integration of Christian Bible teachings and practices, for the improvement of knowledge and understanding of Jesus Christ, in order for us to get rid of worldly things and to become true disciples of the Lord.

The main concept of Christianity stretches from Christian belief in Christ's birth, His Gospel, teachings, death, resurrection, His Second Coming, to the entire Christian work towards Christ's coming.

The Bible

To become true Christians and influence the world, it is essential to have a deep understanding of Christ's birth, His doctrine and teachings as well as  His life. This emphasises the application of the Bible (God's Word), to establish a better relationship between God and His people and our neighbours, and to experience God's presence, His glory and power to affect the world.

What is the *Bible* and what is it all about?

The Bible could be considered as just a book written by some people, prophets or ordinary people, a book that has an input and an outcome. The input refers to the effort put in to live in accordance with biblical requirements, and the outcome is the result of this. The Bible is something written by human beings like us; however, those who wrote it are not considered here. We are only concerned with its content, and the relationship between people and God. It is very important for us to know what the Bible is and all that it is about. It is very sad and surprising that we do not deeply understand the Bible.

Old Testament ← the Bible → New Testament

1.1: The Bible

As diagram 1.1 indicates, the Bible consists of two main matters – the past and the present. The past and present do not necessarily imply that one is out of date, but that the Bible is two books combined. These books are connected and they function together to fulfil one purpose. The purpose is to save the lives of God's people. It is known that the Bible has two parts; however, they may not be separated and condemned, although it may appear that there are some discrepancies in some of the books of the Bible. All the details of the Bible are based on past events and experiences that are likely to lead to things in the future. This concerns the love that we as God's children have for God in our present and future lives.

The Bible is a holy book that is written about the Christian or believers' religion. Holy means that something comes from God and is consecrated to the Lord's service.

This Bible consists of two main books: the Old Testament and the New Testament. The Old Testament is about the Hebrew people, their religion and social laws. In addition, it contains history and the writings of the prophets, as well as important Hebrew literature. The New Testament is concerned with Christianity, which contains within itself the Covenant between God and the Hebrew people, which was established through Moses on Mount Sinai.

Christianity means the Christian religion, taught by Jesus Christ and His followers. This Christianity is about how we fear the Lord, obey Him and trust Him.

In a nutshell, these two holy books, the Old Testament and New Testament, have become one Holy Book, as emphasised by the Lord Jesus Christ. As the Lord said, He did not come to condemn the Old Testament: He came to fulfil it.

What concerns us most is the application of the Bible and our response to it, which allow us to abide with God's Word. The Holy Spirit demonstrates God's meaning in every Christian Life. The question here is how we can know the presence of the Holy Spirit in our lives, and what the Spirit can do for us. For example, when we are in difficulties, we may understand that God has power and authority to overcome such difficulties, therefore we need to focus on God. As Christians, we are called to do what is biblical, before we can demonstrate through our actions and words the truth of the Bible that proclaims God's love, care and peace, to save the lives of God's people in the world. This is a very difficult task and a significant responsibility, because we have to demonstrate this in practical terms, and it takes our love and commitment to do it. There is a real danger that we might proclaim the Gospel without experiencing it ourselves, or knowing its application, and effects. Many of us study the Bible and preach it, but we do not know its rules, applications and effects. We may even not want to know, since we are not concerned about the effect of the Bible in our lives and public life. In fact, if we understood and knew how to apply the Word of God, we would be able to solve problems and save the lives of the people of God.

Fear of God

Fear God and keep His commandments, for this is man's all. (Ecclesiastes 12:13)

Whatever I tell you in the dark, speak in the light; and what you hear in the ear, preach on the housetops. And do not fear those who kill the body but cannot kill the soul. But rather fear Him who is able to destroy both soul and body in hell. (Matthew 10:27–28)

The words *fear God and keep His commandments* here are our whole Gospel duty. To fear God is our submission to God and other people, speaking the truth and keeping our promises. The scriptures above tell us to fear God, because whatever God does shall be forever, and it is God who will bring every work, including every secret thing, to judgement. God is always with His children, He always preserves us; He is our rock, shield and strength. It is only He who provides for us, pardons our sins and guides us. The fear of God does not necessarily mean that if we do not fear Him He will kill us. Fearing God has nothing to do with killing or destroying. It shows that God has all the power and authority, and His presence is everywhere at the same time. Thus, this fear of God is the exaltation of God, because He is omnipotent and omnipresent. In fact, fear of the Lord is humble obedience; it is this humble obedience that we lack. People think that if someone shows humility to them, then the person is stupid or there is something wrong with them. Therefore, they may try to take as much advantage of that person as possible, without realising that humility should be one of the characteristics of a human being, especially ours. We find it very hard to humble ourselves before the Lord, who created us and takes care of us despite all our sins.

There are so many important things about fearing the Lord. The most outstanding things are that it gives strong confidence, and that we will have a *place of refuge* (*Proverbs 14:26*). It is a source of life, and a means of protecting us from death (*Proverbs 14:27*), and it helps us to speak the truth (*Matthew 10:27*) that creates a real and improved relationship with God. In fact, our real relationship with God is the essential aspect of the Gospel. We really need to have such a relationship. It is through this relationship with God that we may succeed in our Gospel ambition. However, it is a very difficult task for us to accomplish, because it is something that deals with purity. God constantly wants us to be purified so that we can have real intimacy with Him. However, because of our lack of commitment and vision, nothing changes in our lives.

Obedience

Obedience is respecting God and doing His will. It is acting in obedience to the rules and orders of God. Surely, the Lord desires obedience from His people, just as all parents desire obedience from their children. Our Christian obedience to God and His work is the response to the call to be genuine Christians. Doing His will means doing what the Bible says. The Word of God says that t*o obey is better than sacrifice (1 Samuel 15:22)*. We cannot be Christians without doing His will.

The Bible tells us that there are true Christians and false Christians. True Christians obey God and have a past and a present life. On the other hand, false Christians do not want to change: they are still the same as when they came to Christ. These Christians do not obey God, neither do they do His work; they think that their position in the Church or contribution to the Church, such as money and work, can make them true Christians.

Trust

Trust is having confidence in God and His Word. It is a firm confidence that God exists and that His Word is true, even though we have not known God nor seen Him physically. Our trust in God means having the strength to keep on going. It is having confidence and not letting our hearts be troubled in hard times, hoping that the Lord will not let us down. It is hoping that some good thing will come out of a bad situation. Trust is being proud of being Christians, since we understand that we are blessed through the blood of the Lord Jesus Christ. It is also depending on God in accordance with His doctrine, rather than depending on ourselves. We Christians should know that the Lord we worship is reliable and responsible for His Word. He is the God who will never forsake us, neither will He leave us, especially in times of trouble.

We struggle, day in and day out, to cope with the world situation, because of lack of knowledge and deep understanding of the Bible and its message. We are all obliged to know about the Bible, to enable us to understand and know the God we worship. We believers are supposed to know our responsibilities and duties to the Lord. The clear understanding of the Bible will easily aid us personally to contribute to our spiritual growth and enable us to cope with the world situation, no matter what happens.

There are many people who proclaim that they are born-again Christians, true disciples of the Lord Jesus Christ, and that they know and deeply understand what the Bible is about, but do not want to act in accordance with it. Is it because they do not understand what the entire Bible is about, or is it because of wealth and achievements that they will leave behind when their lives fade out? As a result, they live contrary to the message and teachings of our Lord Jesus Christ. So it is very important to look at the meaning of the Bible and what it is about!

The Bible was written by holy men, through the inspiration of God, and directed by the Holy Spirit. It is a book written in the Hebrew, Aramaic and Greek languages. The Bible shows the attitude of Jesus Christ our Lord Himself, and the circle of His followers. This book is for us to learn, study and practise, to enable us to follow Him. This Bible is something in which we can have confidence, so that we can place our hope in Him. Truly, we believe that the Bible cannot be broken and nobody, not even an angel of Heaven, could have the authority to correct or modify its message.

The main ideal of the Bible is the work of God in delivering humans from the power of sin and death, through Jesus Christ, our redeemer and deliverer. We, the people of God, are not forced to accept the messages in it. The Bible sets out the Christian doctrine, and we place our hope in it by following Jesus Christ's footsteps. However, declaring that we are born-again Christians and taking the consequences of this, we have to follow in the footsteps of Jesus Christ, our life and His teachings, by believing and practising.

What is the Bible all about?

In the beginning was the Word, and the Word was with God, and the Word was God. He was in the beginning with God. All things were made through Him, and without Him nothing was made that was made. In Him was life, and the life was the light of men. And the light shines in the darkness, and the darkness did not comprehend it. (John1:1–5)

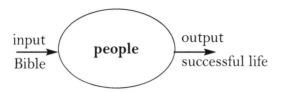

1.2: How the Bible works

According to the Gospel of John above, it could be said that the Bible is simply about life. The Bible demonstrates the things that we can and cannot do, to enable us to achieve the desired life that the Bible refers to. Figure 1.2 above shows the Bible as an input of life that enables us to achieve a better output. The output is the outcome of every child of life on this earth. It does not indicate whether we are rich or poor. It means that we will do the will of God by applying the Bible in our personal lives, enabling us to obtain a successful life. This is the end of life for the people of God, and is vital for everyone. Only by applying the Bible to our lives will we achieve successful lives.

The Bible is the book of the holy writings of the Christian religion. This book deals entirely with God. The statement above from John's Gospel shows us that before everything was created by God, the Word was already there. This Word was with God and the same Word was God, which implies that the Word is God himself and at the same time it refers to the Bible. God who created our people is known as Jesus Christ, who is the Son of God, born of Mary and the Holy Spirit. Thus, the Bible can be considered as God or Jesus Christ, which is life.

As Christians, the question we may ask ourselves is: what is meant by the word life? It refers to anything that is alive. Living things, such as people and animals, grow and reproduce, so we are considering the life of human beings. There are many important factors: food and good health are major ones. Eating the right kinds of food promotes good health and stability that provide a longer life.

A longer life enables us to fulfil the vision which God has given to us.

We believe that God the creator has given each one of us a vision to be fulfilled on this earth, and we cannot to accomplish this vision without eating good food to sustain our life.

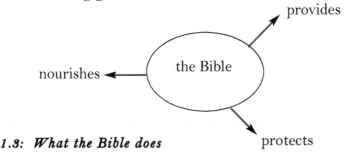

1.3: *What the Bible does*

According to the scriptures above, it could be said in a nutshell that the Bible is life, as it nourishes, provides and protects the people of God, as is depicted in figure 1.3 above. The Bible nourishes us, the people of God, and it keep us alive and well, by feeding us with the necessary ingredients to grow. The Bible provides for us, acting as a source of support, giving what we need, and taking care of us. It saves us from danger by protecting us. It is likely that anyone who fulfils the requirements of the Bible will be successful in life, as figure 1.3 shows.

Most Christians do not have a true sense of the abiding presence of God. The love of God for His people is very precious. He calls us and always wants us to be on a higher level of hard work and commitment by doing His work. God knows which things of the world will lead us astray. The main factors in the Bible are to have a close relationship with God and with one another that is based on love. This relationship is gained through the Ten Commandments. The Commandments are a way of life based on love, as God wants us to do things from our hearts; He is interested in our hearts, minds and our relationship with one another.

Matthew 5:8 states, *Blessed are the pure in heart, for they shall see God.* The goal of every Christian life is to see God; therefore, we have to live a good life in such a way that we will see God, and He will open up the treasure of all blessings for us and provide us with eternal life. This is what the Bible is about.

Features of Life

The features of life deal with the major requirements of life, growth and reproduction.

Growth

Growth applies to all Christians, both in our physical and spiritual lives. We all expect to grow both physically and spiritually. However, here we are not concerned with physical growth. Our main concern is spiritual growth because this is what interests God. It allows us to do the work of God. In fact, it is certain that anyone who wants to abide with the Gospel has to aim for spiritual growth, for otherwise we will forget the Gospel. This is because the world is full of wrath and woes, which are contrary to the Word of God. If we genuinely do God's work, then we will grow spiritually.

There are so many people doing God's work, but the question is: are we doing genuine work, and are we genuine Christians? Christians now are slaves of sin, and our Christian souls are now full of troubles. Therefore, we cannot call daily upon God, because our sins are many and our wickedness is great. It is well known that Christians are supposed to gain hearts of wisdom, and this wisdom comes from God and from doing God's work. The major problem of Christianity is that some of us do not want to know God's Word, and do not seek to let God's Word appear to us, and do not keep ourselves in all God's ways with the help of God's angels.

Reproduction

This refers to the process by which we human beings produce individuals like us, and is a very important feature of human life. Without growth and reproduction, human life would be impossible. It is very necessary for all of us Christians to wish to produce our kind of children. Although some people cannot reproduce, they still have life.

However, are we Christians aiming to let God teach us to serve Him with complete devotion? If we do this, we will be able to produce our own kind, by the grace of God. How can we wish to produce our own kind without aiming to do God's work?

In fact, God knows our thoughts, whether our thought is to seek God's Kingdom or our own prosperity by any means. Many of us think that God answers prayers, so we call to Him in times of trouble or we call for forgiveness when we have intentionally sinned. We believe strongly that sin is sin, therefore as Christians, we are not supposed to sin. We know that sin is totally against the Gospel. If we are aware that we are the slave of a particular sin, and we commit that sin, it is against our Gospel. If we sin, we need to fast, and ask for forgiveness for all our wrongs. We need to seek God's Kingdom, so that God will use us and give us great victory in His love, making us triumphant in every area in our lives.

Types of Life

And the LORD God formed man of the dust of the ground, and breathed into his nostrils the breath of life; and man became a living being. (Genesis 2:7)

Mostly assuredly, I say to you, he who hears My word and believes in Him who sent Me has everlasting life, and shall not come into judgment, but has passed from death into life. (John 5:24)

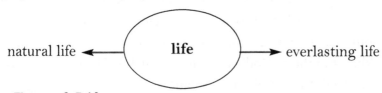

natural life ⟵ **life** ⟶ everlasting life

1.4: Types of Life

The books of Genesis and John tell us that there are two main types of life as shown in figure 1.4: one is called *natural life* (physical life) and the other one is everlasting or *eternal life* (spiritual life). Natural life refers to the animate part of man, a life inherited from Adam. Natural life is the life on this earth that every child of God is born into, the common life of humankind, experienced by all. Natural life consists of two lives, which are 'long life' and 'short life'.

The causes of long and short lives are believed to depend on the Creator's will, and can also depend on ourselves because of our life or character. It is not the will of God to create His children to live on this earth to fulfil His vision and then to live a very short life. The causes of death of some people are very sad and not understood, but it is doubtful that God who loves His people can let things like that happen.

Everlasting or *eternal life* is simply means *life after death.* This is the type of life to which the scriptures refer. Death is defined as the ending of the life of a person. Death is also the power to destroy our life, anywhere and any time.

There are two kinds of body according to the book of 1 *Corinthians 15:42–3.* The natural body is sown in *corruption…dishonour… weakne*ss. This body is not raised differently as compared to the spiritual; however, it bears spiritual fruit. The natural body is considered to be our first body, associated with the flesh and is made of dust; a person then becomes a living being as a child of God.

The spiritual body is a body that rises from the natural dead body. It is believed that this kind of body is raised in *corruption… glory…power.* It usually becomes a life-giving spirit and bears the image of the heavenly person.

Life after death means that when we die, our body, which is known as earth, will go back to its original soil. Our soul may still have life. This soul has two chances: one is to go to God who creates humankind, to inherit God's Kingdom, which is Heaven. The other is to go to Hell, the kingdom of Satan.

Life after death is the most important aspect of human life, especially for Christians. It can be said that life after death is what we are always working hard to achieve. Life after death is so important that the Bible, which is the Word of God, was written for the people of God to study and put into practice, so that we will be able to achieve this kind of life before we die. Life after death can also be considered as a bonus of life, showing the achievement of God and His Gospel. It actually demonstrates the love of God for His people and the outcome of Jesus Christ's coming, and His death on the Cross of Calvary. It is a bonus of life because it is given freely, without payment from anyone. God provides it to His people through the will of Jesus Christ to die for our sins. However, the assessment of our lives is based on our Gospel work, and our whole life on this earth may decide whether or not we are entitled to life after death. The character of God's people is believed to be the main factor in this assessment. So what are we, the people of God, doing about it? Life after death, commonly known as Spiritual Life, surpasses and is more valuable than everything else on this earth.

Difference between Natural Life and Everlasting Life

Everlasting life is the type of life that can only be experienced after we die, the life of God, which is given to all believers in Jesus Christ. This type of life is something that comes from believing (*John 6:47*). It is commonly believed that not all of us have the chance to experience this kind of life. Everlasting life is something that may come out of love, the acceptance of Jesus Christ as the Son of God and as one personal Saviour, and doing His Gospel work.

The main difference between natural and everlasting life is that everlasting life deals with spiritual life and has nothing to do with death, and is the greatest gift that God gives to His people. The condition is that the people of God have to fulfil it and may qualify from a natural life-assessment by God. This life- assessment determines who is entitled to have this everlasting life; it is known and done by God alone. Nobody knows the condition of life after death except the Maker Himself. However, it seems that it will be totally different from natural life here on this earth.

Natural life has been described as a democratic life. We can all do whatever we like, good things or bad. It may involve many things that are not good for human life; it is full of woes and is actually to do with death.

Features of the Bible

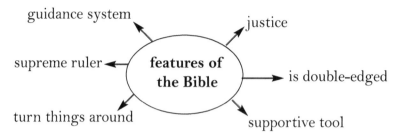

1.5: Features of the Bible

The features of the Bible refer to what the Word of God is and what it can do. The outcome of the Bible depends on these features which show us the love that God has for His people, and His willingness to do things for us and to protect us.

Therefore, it is vital for us to concentrate on the Bible rather than anything else, since other things will do nothing for us in the end. Looking at figure 1.5, we see that there is nothing that the Bible cannot do. Frankly, it promotes sure success and it is a wonder of nature. It cannot be changed, neither is it subject to any modification. Events in the Bible are in accordance with the facts of nature and natural laws. The most outstanding features of the Bible are as follows:

Supreme ruler

It is a supreme ruler with great power over everything. No one, regardless of nationality, position, personality, gender and colour, can surpass it.

Guidance system

It is a guidance system for the management and control of everything on earth, especially human beings. It advises, manages and controls humankind's complex situation, such as protecting and preventing people from danger and destruction.

Justice

It performs in accordance with its principle and process of justice, in order to promote peace. God loves and values everybody, regardless of personality and circumstances, because we all have value and are all equal in human worth. Therefore, God is justice and is always on the side of justice towards His world. God created everyone in His own image and he loves His children; He does not favour anybody specially, and His Word is justice. The Bible here demonstrates the principles of good practice, equality and non-discrimination.

It is double-edged

It is a double-edged weapon or tool, making use of both edges. With everybody, it can destroy life and give life, actually demonstrating the potential and the truth of the Gospel.

It supports people in time of trouble, and it supplies the necessities of life. The Word of God always stands against the danger posed by the evil of others to the people of God. It acts as a resource for all of us, and supports us in times of need, enabling us to cope with problems and difficulties.

It turns things around

It has power to turn things around at any time. The Word of God can make a terrible situation good, and the other way around too.

Importance of the Bible

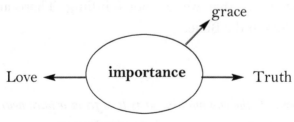

1.6: Importance of the Bible

The importance of the Bible is more necessary than anything else; otherwise,, the Bible might be considered as useless. It is this importance of the Bible that we do not know or even think about. It is very sad that we do not value it. This is a serious problem in the church of God today; going to church has become more important for us than applying what the Bible says to our lives and cleaning up the clutter. Since we do not have a clue about the importance of the Bible, nothing has changed for ages in the church of God.

There is something in us today that makes us ignorant about the Gospel of Christ: we do lots of fasting, praying and reading the Bible. However, we do not apply the Word to our lives. Our approach to God is to get what we need, but we refuse to commit anything to God in return. The sad thing about us is that we do not know and understand the importance of the Bible and our duties as Christians. It is totally naïve for us to think that God does not require anything from us. We should understand that we have a contract: we have responsibilities to perform in order to fulfil the agreement. Truly, without any fulfilment of the agreement, it is very hard to experience the presence of God and the benefits of the Gospel.

We should bear in mind that the Gospel was not just given to the people of God. There is a reason and purpose for this. God always sees His people standing far from Him, while He wants us to draw near to Him so that we can be saved. The purpose of God for His people cannot be achieved without us drawing near to Him. Therefore, the Bible and God's son Jesus were God's means of getting His people near Him, to enable Him to fulfil His purpose. At the same time, God requires some responsibility from His people; it is this responsibility that we are not fulfilling. There are many important factors in the Bible:

Love

Now the purpose of the commandment is love from a pure heart, from a good conscience, and from sincere faith. (1 Timothy 1:5)

16

This *love* was given through Moses in the Old Testament, and is the most outstanding concept in the Bible. In the book of Exodus, Moses was appointed by God to lead the Israelites out of slavery in Egypt, from the hands of King Pharaoh and the Egyptians. They travelled through the desert and crossed the Red Sea. Then they based themselves at Mount Sinai, where God gave the Ten Commandments to Moses.

These Ten Commandments are:

1. I am the Lord your God, who brought you out of the land of Egypt, out of the house of bondage. You shall have no other gods before Me.

2. You shall not make for yourself a carved image—any likeness of anything that is in heaven above, or that is in the earth beneath, or that is in the water under the earth; you shall not bow down to them nor serve them. For I, the Lord your God, am a jealous God, visiting the iniquity of the fathers upon the children to the third and fourth generations of those who hate Me, but showing mercy to thousands, to those who love Me and keep My commandments.

3. You shall not take the name of the Lord your God in vain, for the Lord will not hold him guiltless who takes His name in vain.

4. Remember the Sabbath day, to keep it holy. Six days you shall labour and do all your work, but the seventh day is the Sabbath of the Lord your God. In it you shall do no work: you, nor your son, nor your daughter, nor your male servant, nor your female servant, nor your cattle, nor your stranger who is within your gates. For in six days the Lord made the heavens and the earth, the sea, and all that is in them, and rested the seventh day. Therefore the Lord blessed the Sabbath day and hallowed it.

5. Honour your father and your mother, that your days may be long upon the land which the Lord your God is giving you.

6. You shall not murder.

7. You shall not commit adultery.

8. You shall not steal.

9. You shall not bear false witness against your neighbour.

10. You shall not covet your neighbour's house; you shall not covet your neighbour's wife, nor his male servant, nor his female servant, nor his ox, nor his donkey, nor anything that is your neighbour's. (*Exodus 20:2–17*)

In fact, without love, there would be no commandments, because the purpose of the commandments is love. Jesus Christ came by means of love. Love surpasses all things; for us to be able to keep the commandments of God and to fulfil and obey the truth, we have to love one another. Therefore, as is clear from the scripture above, we cannot fulfil the commandment without having love for one another. Loving one another is the same as loving God; this will allow our Christian vision to be accomplished.

Grace

…the laws were given through Moses, but grace and truth came through Jesus Christ. (John 1:17)

Jesus Christ entered into a covenant of grace with us, in order to deliver us from sin and misery. It is this grace that allowed Jesus Christ to bring His children to salvation, and it was achieved through redemption. The Lord Jesus Christ offered Himself up as a sacrifice to divine justice and reconciled His children to God the Father; he also intercedes for us. This grace is given to us as children of God, allowing us to follow Christ. Therefore, without grace, nobody would be able to follow God. In fact, grace acts as a means of accepting Jesus Christ and following Him.

Truth

Jesus said to him, I am the way, the truth, and the life. No one comes to the father except through Me. (John 14:6)

According to this scripture, the truth emphasises the reality of the Lord Jesus Christ. This reality is about the facts and true nature of Jesus, His Gospel and teachings as well as His relationship with God. In fact, it deals with the identity and destiny of Jesus Christ. It shows us that Jesus Christ was and is the Son of God, who became human and redeemed God's people from sin, and who still intercedes for us.

2 Believers

Introduction

In order to analyse how we can change ourselves and the world, the Gospel is necessary. It is the main factor determining the outcome of believers, and distinguishes them from others. It shows our relationship with God and with our neighbours. The basis for the Gospel is provided by both spiritual and physical laws governing believers' behaviour. This chapter will consider different types of believers, including Christians, non-Christians, backsliders, followers and unbelievers. It will explore the understanding of the Gospel, along with belief in it and also different interpretations of it, to provide practical aspects of Christian living and allow a better relationship with God and with each other, and so to influence the world.

Believers are people who think that something is real or true. Believers accept the existence of something with or without certainty, and have faith in that particular thing. Thus, for example, some people may believe that the Earth is flat, rather than spherical. There is a relationship between it and these people. The believers are interested in this relationship and wish to keep it, demonstrating this through their words and actions. Through learning and studying the Earth, some changes occur in the lives of these believers, and so, through their faith, these people are transformed from their old nature to a new nature.

Types of Believers

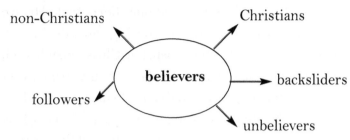

2.1: Types of Believers

Christians

Beware of false prophets, who come to you in sheep's clothing, but inwardly they are ravenous wolves. You will know them by their fruits. Do men gather grapes from thornbushes or figs from thistles? (Matthew 7:15–16)

What are Christians and, in particular, who are Christians?

Christians are in a relationship with God and with one another. We live our lives through the Ten Commandments, a way of life based on love. God is interested in our hearts and minds, and in our relationship with one another, therefore God wants us to do things from our heart. This relationship with God and each other will allow us to inherit God's Kingdom.

We believe in and agree to follow Jesus Christ, by doing the work of God, which is the Gospel. We accept Jesus Christ as the Son of God, the Saviour, His teachings and Gospel, and we make the decision to do His work. It is about how we love God, put our faith in Him and work hard. It is about our firm hope in God, and our understanding that God loves us and has chosen us to be His own. It is letting the news of our faith in God and His Gospel go everywhere in the world.

We act from an agreement to study and learn the Gospel, and do the same things as Christ. We belong to an organisation that has rules and regulations to enable it to function. We, its members, have to obey the rules if we want the organisation to grow; we and others benefit from it. However, our main function depends on God, and so do the benefits of being Christians and our efforts to do His work.

Being Christians means that we are working towards the religion of Christ, which can be called the Gospel or Christ-membership. If we want to become full and active members of any group, we need to fulfil our duties and obligations to that particular group. The same thing applies to Christians wanting to be part of the Christian religion. This religion has nothing to do with worldly matters, but with spiritual matters; it refers to the Kingdom of God and its inheritance.

We are people who want to offer ourselves to serve God, and to be used for the advancement of His Kingdom across the world. This advancement does not necessarily mean the establishing of many Christian churches, or organising Christian crusades. It is to do with the knowledge of the life of Christ and His teachings and how they impact the lives of other people.

We have agreed to study and learn God's Word, and put it into practice. It allows us to understand that everyone has value, because God values each one of us equally in human worth and in dignity.

Being Christians through baptism, we make an agreement to do Christian work. This work is the Gospel, and it is in doing this work that we become Christians. If we agree to do Christian work and are baptised, and then after the baptism are unable to fulfil this work, we cannot be considered as Christians.

Who are Christians?

Then Jesus said to those Jews who believed Him, "If you abide in my Word, you are My disciples indeed. And you shall know the truth and the truth shall make you free. "(John 8:31–32)
Looking at the scripture above, we see that the term Christian is used to describe people who do Christian work. This means Gospel work, referring to the life of Christ and His teachings. We try to live in union with God, keeping our roots and building our life in Him, to become stronger in our personal faith, in order to have peace and

thanksgiving in the Holy Spirit.

We have received a new life, which is the life of God, and we are constantly trying to keep to this new life, getting rid of old sins. We have two lives: our past life and our new life. We believe that it is God who has given us new life, through baptism, as result of repentance and the acceptance of Jesus Christ as our personal Saviour. Therefore, we are always trying to continue with our new life and not go back to our past life. We believe that our past life did not and never will do us any good.

We are Gospel learners, understanding the need to be grounded in God's Word, to equip us for the Gospel work. We believe in the Word of God and put it into practice all the time. We are aware that we bear a responsibility to proclaim and demonstrate the truth of the Gospel through our words and actions; therefore, we have to abide in the Word of God to achieve this vision. Our main aim is to have everlasting life, as a result of doing the work of God in this world; therefore, we worship, obey and love God.

We understand that we must abide in God's Word. The word 'abide' means to continue doing God's work. We always focus on God's Word and do His work, regardless of circumstances. We have faith in Christ and His teachings. We support and promote the Christian Gospel, encouraging people to be part of it. We constantly demonstrate that in Christ there is peace and an understanding of the love of God for all His children.

We believe that, in the world, we have a significant responsibility to demonstrate in a practical manner our love and commitment to save the lives of people. We are concerned with the Gospel and the effect that it has on us and our neighbours. Therefore, we are always interested in Bible study, loving people and encouraging them to turn to God.

We have received the Lord Jesus Christ as our personal Saviour through baptism. This means that we have received a new life – the life of Christ. Receiving a new life does not mean that we can do whatever we want to do. Neither can we continue in sin, as during our past, just because we are Christians and because God will always forgive us. We have made the decision to follow Jesus Christ. Therefore, it is our duty to make all the necessary changes in our life, in order to adopt this new life system, which is the life of Christ.

We have both our old nature and our new nature. Our past is our old nature, and our present is our new nature. We have turned away from our old nature to God, and we have agreed to put away these old bad things. With God's assistance, our life has been filled with good things through baptism. We have become a new creation, we have become Christians. Everything about us has become new, so our life is now different from the past. Therefore, we cannot do past things again after accepting Christ as our personal Saviour through baptism. The new life that we have received is for ever. Since we have accepted the Lord, we must put on good things, instead of putting on bad things, like our past malpractices. To become genuine Christians, we need to have knowledge and wisdom, and put this into practice. We always focus on God and His Gospel. We constantly aim to work with other people, even if there are problems, instead of backbiting and fighting each other for personal achievement or position.

Our life is concerned with repentance, and this helps us to continue to do the work of God. We have repented of our sins and turned from them, with a desire to make restoration, by living a new life, which is the life of God. We do what is right, we are filled with God's knowledge, we are controlled by the Holy Spirit, and always aim to be more like the Lord Jesus Christ.

We are called to follow Christ; however, because of human nature, we sometimes do not follow the teachings of God. This occurs when we do something un-biblical, which means that we are not yet genuine in our Christianity. As humans, we are associated with sin, and this sin always pulls us from our new life back to our old life. However, we are working towards being followers of Christ.

Being Christians

Jesus Christ said that if we abide in His Word, we are His disciples indeed. This means that it is only those who do the work of God who can be called Christians. Many people of God think that Christians are people who have accepted Jesus as their personal Saviour, who always go to church and are involved in church activities. These activities are events planned by a church, involving the work of God, but doing them does not make people Christians. These activities let us understand that we are in a different area of life, and they help us focus on God by applying the Word of God in our lives. They actually encourage us to remain in our new life, so that we should not go back again to where we were, doing things that are contrary to God's Word; this is normally described as being in darkness.

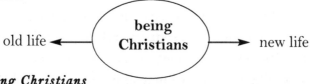

old life ← being Christians → new life

2.2: Being Christians

The old life is the life we lived before we came to Christ, before we knew Christ as our personal Saviour. We have realised that this old life was not doing us any good; in this old life, we could do whatever we wanted. If we did not get rid of this old life, there was no way for us to succeed.

With the new life, there is a change of life. A change of life means we have turned away from our old life to a new life. We have rid ourselves of all the sins that no one knows and all the sins that everyone knows, and we have put on a new life. We have been freed from the power of sin. We were buried with Christ, and are also raised with Christ, through our faith in the active power of God, who raised us from death. We understand that we now have a new nature, therefore we are always willing to turn to God for a better life, instead of turning back to sin. We are determined to be learners of God, because we do not want wealth to turn us away from God.

We know and understand the consequence of being blind, so we wish to be taught and led by God, to enable us to lead others who are blind or those who are from our past lives.

Believing and practising

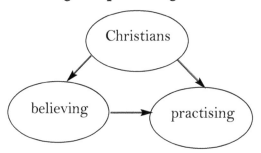

2.3: Basic Elements of our Christian Life

In order for us to change ourselves so that we can influence the people in the world, both of these elements above must be applied in our lives. These elements represent the relationship between our efforts and results. These elements must be considered at every moment in daily life, because we may assist someone to become a Christian. Truly, it is impossible for anyone to become a Christian without believing and practising God's Word. We can only turn away from our past life and put on a new life through believing and practising. Thus it is possible for us children of God to fulfil our Gospel aim, since these words link together to achieve one goal. Only through believing and practising will we understand our Christian expectations.

'Believe' is a synonym for having faith. The verses in the book of *John 3:15–16* make it clear that eternal life is given to those who believe in Jesus Christ as the Son of God, Saviour and Lord: *For God so loved the world that He gave His one and only Son, that everyone who believes in Him shall not perish but have eternal life.* In the Old Testament, when people believed in God, it was accounted to them as righteousness. Believers are those who believe or have persistent faith in Jesus Christ. If we say that we believe in Jesus Christ, then we have to put into operation the power and authority of the

Kingdom of God that we have received through Jesus Christ, to build and strengthen our bodies physically and spiritually. We should have faith in the Lord and our new life, and believe that we can improve our lives and influence the people around us. We must think that we are effective enough to improve our lives. We must be aware that the Lord is always on our side, so what we need to do is only minor action. We must have the ability to stand in the presence of the Lord, without any sense of guilt that prevents us from breaking through any crisis in our lives. Furthermore, we must have faith in the Lord, in order to remain happy and stable in all situations.

Practising is the act of putting Jesus Christ's life and teachings (the Word of God) into action, not just speaking the words. Practising the Word of God will enable us to hear Him speaking to us through the Holy Spirit, to strengthen our faith in Him. Therefore it is very important to put the words of God that we hear or read into practice always, with the full commitment of our hearts. This will help us to know the Lord we are worshipping; it will build our faith, so that we can have confidence in Him and do spectacular things.

Instead of using both our head and heart, many of us use only our head in our approach to the Word of God, thinking that this will lead us to spiritual growth. We may have been part of the body of Jesus Christ for a long time, but we show no sign of spiritual growth. Why? Although our head is very important in our approach to the God's Word, it is vitally important to understand that head-knowledge without heart-commitment will not lead to spiritual growth. Our spirits can only grow by approaching the Word of God with heart-commitment.

These days, we always look for spectacular power through God's Word, without knowing the innate power of the word. It is necessary for believers to understand that God's Word is supernatural, or spiritual. If we are looking for spectacular power, we must first know the innate power of God's Word, and constantly practise it. Practising the Word is the key to achieving spectacular power or doing spectacular things. If we do not want to apply the Word of life into our lives, how can we expect wonders and miracles? How can we achieve what we are looking for? If our aim is to look for spectacular power, then we have to forget about focusing on physical materials, and put God's Word into practice. We need to increase our spiritual growth in order to achieve our aims. If we hear or read the Word of God and do not act on it, then of course we will forget it. However, if we act on the Word with heart-commitment after hearing or reading, this will lead to our spiritual growth, and it will always be with us. As a result, we can expect spectacular power from it.

One overriding advantage of believing and practising is that we can know the presence and power of God. We can concentrate on the Lord by fearing Him and obeying His Commandments. The Commandments are the ten rules for living and for worshipping that God made for Moses on Mount Sinai, for the people of God to follow. Christianity is basically the beliefs and practices of disciples of Jesus Christ, based on His life and teachings. Christianity is not merely a philosophy but is uniquely based on the resurrection of Jesus as a historical fact. If we strongly declare that this fact is true, then Jesus Christ and His teachings have a great claim on our lives. Also, if we believe that we are disciples of Jesus Christ, we have to follow in His footsteps and go through what He went through. The most vital aspect of our Christian life is our relationship with the Word of God, which enables us to be saved and healed.

Elements of our Christian Life

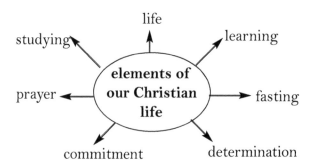

2.4: Elements of our Christian Life

Figure 2.4 above adds more practical and physical details to the elements in figure 2.3. They should also help readers understand the ambitions and expectations of being Christians. These individual elements of our Christian life function differently, but work together to achieve one goal. If there is any separation in these elements, or if we fail to dedicate time to any one element, then there may be a different result. These elements act as the input; they equip us and help our spiritual growth. The combination of these elements will change our lives for the better, and determine what type of believers we are. We control our daily work and decided whether to walk in the way of the Lord all the days of our life, although the Holy Spirit has the overall power. We should be dedicated to all these elements in order to become genuine and effective.

Prayer is the act of speaking to God, for help, peace, and forgiveness. Prayer is the master key for forgiveness, which would otherwise remain unuttered. Prayer is the response to God, and when we pray to God, He responds to us. This response indicates the presence of God, His power and His care. It also makes our praying meaningful. Prayer is a conversation, or intercession, with God to forgive our sins. It also enables us to forgive the mistakes and sins of our sisters and brothers. Prayer equips us to do Gospel work.

Sin is the breaking of God's laws on purpose; it is wrongdoing of any kind, such as stealing, lying, dishonesty and immoral acts. Sin always disturbs our attention to God, especially our attention to the Gospel. This causes a huge blow to our spiritual growth and drags us away from experiencing God's presence, His love and power and all the blessings of the Gospel. Sin prevents our spiritual progress, because the function of the Word of God is based on religious principles. These are the conditions by which the Word of God works. If we sin, our relationship with God is disconnected or blocked; our wilfulness keeps us spiritually apart from God. In accordance with religious principles, nothing can happen between us sinners and God, no matter what we do. Our relationship is blocked until we repent, ask God to forgive what we have done, and refrain from committing that sin.

Prayer is also a form of worship, offered to God to assist us in situations of crisis. The prayer of faith is addressed to a situation, using Jesus' Name based on a specific biblical promise. Truly, there is nothing that prayer cannot do. Praying to God with faith will assist us in overcoming every difficult situation, and allow us to break through to fulfil our mission with the help of the Holy Spirit.
Studying the Bible and reading carefully will allow the Holy Spirit to assist us in understanding the Word of God deeply. Studying helps us make some corrections of our mistakes and errors.

Learning is obtaining knowledge or skills, which enables us to do the work of God and follow in the footsteps of Jesus Christ. If we learn and try to remember what we learn, it opens a way to prosperity. As Christians, we are blessed when we do what is fair and right. How can we do these things without learning and remembering? Learning enables us to speak to God as well as to other people. It helps us to pray, read the Word of God and to confess our sins. The most important thing about learning is that it allows us to open ourselves to God and let God come into our life.
Fasting helps us to lose weight, it enables us to have control over difficulties, and to overcome problems in life. Fasting is also a petition to Almighty God to have mercy on us for wrong things we have done, or to ask God to come to our aid. Fasting is also considered to be one of the major Gospel keys that breaks every yoke and opens golden doors in our life. It allows us to come under the control of the Spirit, and gives us the ability to communicate intimately with God. Fasting makes our voice heard on high to Almighty God. It is a means of drawing God's attention to our needs. Fasting deals with humility and a focus on the Word of God. Its aim is to help us get away from malpractice, to enable the Holy Spirit to have absolute

control of our life. Fasting is also part of worshipping God. Fasting does not necessarily make us Christians, as many people think, but is a means of submitting to God, asking for breakthrough or forgiveness. If we continue fasting without putting the Word of God into practice, then the fasting is in vain. Fasting should always promote spiritual growth and breakthrough.

Determination is when we make up our mind firmly to carry out our purpose. Determination is essential because it opens way for progress, which leads us to success. It is one of the most important ways in which we can take care of the Word of God, to achieve a successful result. Consequently, our determination to follow the Lord should not be weakened by any difficulty. Determination helps us get rid of any doubt which can deal a huge blow to our progress; this is because we always have doubts about our strength and ability to do things as well as God's own ability to do His work or fulfil His promises. We find it very difficult to do some things, because of lack of determination and commitment in our life. However, as Christians, we should not be doubtful about these things, since doubt damages everything that we wish to do, and destroys everything that we ask of God.

We have to be positive and persistent, and have faith in whatever we do, because the Bible tells us that we have the ability to do all things. It is possible for us to handle anything through the Lord; the only thing we must be is determined and committed to the things we do. Commitment is a sign of promise and an indication of what may be expected from us. Christianity is a contract, a mutual agreement between ourselves and God. It is the responsibility of both sides to fulfil the terms of the contract, so our side of this is to do God's work, if we are to experience the benefits of the contract and achieve the Gospel ambition. It is a biblical truth that God always fulfils His duties under this contract. This contractual duty cannot be done all at once: God expects us to do it step by step, through our own willing commitment. The Lord who creates every human being knows that

His people are not as perfect as He is; therefore He does not judge or depend on our spirituality, but simply our willing commitment. He knows that whatever we do, we will all fall into sin one day. It is our commitment that makes us honest. It is our willingness and commitment to do our Gospel work that interests the Lord, because this is proof of our Christian seriousness.

We should follow in the footsteps of Christ and His teachings, to pay for His labour for us. If we look at what Christ has done for us, He has to be paid well. Truly, there is no way that we can pay for what He has done for us other than doing His work sincerely. Jesus Christ was a determined worker; he did not sit back with His arms folded, waiting for things to be done. He fought and fought until a victory was achieved. As His disciples, we are supposed to do the same things, so long as we believe in Him. The Lord's domination has to be faced and accepted by all His people, so that we do not do the things that we wish, but do the will of God.

Advantages of the Elements of our Christian Life

These are the keywords that contribute to our Christian achievement. They are there for our good and bring great benefit to all of us. These advantages are: *learning, studying, believing and practising.* Anyone who wishes to be successful in life and belong to the family of God should focus on these words. We may be busy doing other work of God, thinking that doing this other work classifies us as disciples. Other work cannot take us anywhere, no matter what we do, without our involvement in these key practices. Jesus' disciples can be taken as typical examples of this practice. As human beings, some of His disciples, at certain times, had doubts about some things that Christ was doing.

Learning allows us to know and understand things, and how to deal with them. It helps us to acquire skills and knowledge, and to grow physically and spiritually.

There is a problem, however, involving the deep understanding of the Word, and how much we apply or act on it. This causes many problems that damage the Gospel and the people of God. In order to obtain our attention, some people use unsound or false arguments to teach others. This leads to crisis and separation in the body of Christ, since some of us lack the control of the Holy Spirit in our daily life.

Being Christians mean that we are working towards the religion of Christ, which can be called Gospel- or Christ-membership. Some do not belong to the religion of Christ, and try to thwart our achievement. Religion does not refer to the Christian church or activities, nor does it refer to our Christian position, personality or ability. It has nothing to do with worldly things, but with spiritual things. It refers to the Kingdom of God. We Christians are people who want to offer ourselves to God, and to serve and be used spiritually, for the advancement of His Kingdom across the world.

Studying lets us understand and remember things better, examine them and add value to them. When we learn, study and apply things, we will be able to stand against dangers and opposition from the enemy.

Believing: as the proverb goes, seeing is believing. Belief in God and reliance on Him has become our biggest problem. With all the efforts that we put into Gospel work, it seems there is nothing new for us, that there is no fruit from our Christian doings, both physical and spiritual. Why be Christians, if we do not get anything out of it? Naturally, we do not get money or property. We receive the assurance that God loves and cares for us. It demonstrates to us, both physically and spiritually, that God is the only one who can see us throughout our life. We have the assurance of God's presence and power above all things.

Sometimes, the main 'bread' of Jesus Christ is neglected, because of our personal belongings or needs, which means that our inner spirit is not receiving the bread that lasts forever. It is mostly the lack of belief and the poor teaching of the Gospel that cause

Christian poverty. The main question here is how we can believe something that we have not seen. However, it is only belief in the Word and putting it into practice that will let a person knows its truth. Belief helps us have confidence in God and proclaim the kindness of God.

Practising provides more experience and improvement, and encourages growth, both physical and spiritual. Practising the Word of God changes our life and lets us experience God's presence and His power; we may do what others do not see or do; these practices will enable God to prevail in our mind. However, problems can arise if there are important things to get or do in our life as we. This could cause us to do something that will be contrary to the Bible, and lead us to betray Christ; it could even lead some people into trouble, or we could risk our entire lives.

Elements of Christian Development

These are the things that help us develop and grow in our faith in God. The Lord has called us into His ministry to be faithful, so that the seed in us will grow and bear good fruit. In fact, we all have a seed, which is so powerful; but it needs other elements to assist its growth. We must stand fast in the Lord so that we will not be tossed about with the many conflicts of the world.

These elements are at times known as Christian responsibilities. It is our faith and our practice of the Word that makes us Christians, and that also leads us to being disciples and successful in our lives. It is essential for us to continue to develop and grow in this faith that made us Christians, since, at times, the pressures of the world or Christian circumstances can make us feel faithless, miserable or unsuccessful in life. These problems concerning our Christianity and our lives always influence us. Because of this, we need the grace of God and people supporting us, to help us stand against any challenges. Some of us think that as soon as we become Christians, this is the end of problems, and that there will be nothing we need do, since God will take control of us and our needs.

There is a difference between *Christians* and *churchgoers*. Being Christian is a commitment for life and it depends on us ourselves; being a churchgoer, however, is for a specified length of time. God calls all Christians, and this call can come through us ourselves or through another person. However the call happens, we become Christians. The important thing is that God calls us to become part of His ministry. Being members of God's ministry means that we have put on a new life and put our old life behind us; we have decided to work towards God's life.

As Christians, we should be able to build a great and strong relationship with God, and we cannot do this without responsibilities. So, what are these Christian responsibilities and what happens if these responsibilities are not carried out?

Christian Responsibilities

*Christian responsibilitie*s are the things that we should know and the work that we should do. As Christians, we have an obligation to understand our responsibilities, so that we will know what to do and what not to do. This will allow us to use the good things of the Gospel. In addition, the benefits and rewards of the Gospel actually depend on us. The only way to accomplish our Gospel goal is to fulfil our responsibilities.

How important is our role in Christ's ministry? Carrying out these Christian responsibilities depends on commitment and self-reliance.

Commitment is the process of doing something. It is valuable in the Gospel and our Christian life because without it, we will not be able to fulfil our Christian work. As soon as we become Christians, we commit ourselves to doing the work of God. This is a great promise to God, who looks forward to us fulfilling it. The Lord knows that only those of us who are honest will fulfil our promise, since there are many challenges making it difficult for us to accomplish it. It is commitment and hard work that will enable us to fulfil our task.

Being followers of Christ usually means continuing to do the work of God with a genuine heart, so we can positively respond to our call to be Christians.

Self-reliance means that we depend on own efforts. Though God is there for everybody, it is our own effort that will make us fulfil our promise. In fact, God is always willing to assist His people in every way so that His name will be glorified. What happens if we are not willing or prepared to do anything? We cannot be forced by God to do anything; Christianity does not force people to accept Christ and worship Him.

Truly, following God's Word with commitment and self-reliance will give us valuable insight into the Gospel, in order to save people's lives. As Christians, we should understand and know what we need and actually manage it, so that we can offer this to others and save them. We will progress by rooting and grounding ourselves in Christ. We cannot be thus rooted and built up without carrying out our responsibilities. We are supposed to go elsewhere and share our beliefs. Nothing can enable us to respond to this task except doing it, and then progressing in it, in order to develop and grow in faith.

These Christian responsibilities allow us to stand firm during any changes in the world. We should be willing to commit ourselves to carrying out these responsibilities, regardless of the circumstances. The Lord who calls us knows that we have potential, and He has seen us as potential Christians doing His work. At times, however, there will be problems for us to go through, which will influence our development and our growing faith in God. However, since it is our duty and responsibility to learn and study, to believe and practise the Word of God, we have no choice other than to fulfil our Christian responsibilities.

We hold the most responsible Gospel position on this Earth. All of us are responsible for the care of the Gospel and the children of God. We cannot fulfil our Gospel goals if we do not know our responsibilities. It is we who have to undertake the Gospel role and play any possible part we can, to save the people of God who are in darkness. This Christian duty is the way in which God assesses our work.

In fact, being Christians is not as easy as it seems. It is not only constantly going to church, nor is it an overnight job. We are people who understand and believe that no weapons can withstand us. We have reason to believe that nothing can stand against us, despite all the problems we go through. Our reward is that we are the fruit of God's suffering. God loves us, has redeemed us, and has saved us from suffering. The Lord has given us peace and joy, so that whatever happens to us is just temporary.

We who call ourselves followers of Christ sometimes do our own thing. Strange things happen and baffle us, so that we doubt the existence and presence of God. The public feel sorry for us, instead of us feeling sorry for ourselves. We struggle to get answers to these problems, thinking that going to church every moment and fasting can both help. We try to think our own way out of these troubles, but still the problems remain, or even increase. Since we do not know our responsibilities, we cannot get rest. We do not realise that we have been given some responsibilities through our restoration from sin by the blood of Jesus Christ.

These responsibilities are to fear, trust and obey God, and are the main work of Christians. It is the fulfilment of these responsibilities that can make us Christians, because it will help us put off the old things, in order to focus on the Word of God and work towards the life of Christ. It is necessary for us to perform these tasks, although simply doing them will not make us Christians. However, they help us develop and grow in faith in God, which enables us to accomplish our Christian ambition.

Factors that cannot make us Christians

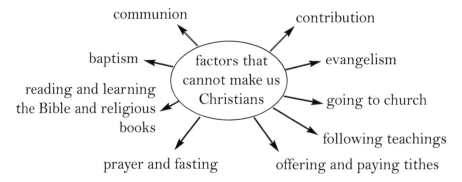

2.5: Factors that cannot make us Christians

Apart from the change from an old to a new life that makes us good Christians, other factors in figure 2.5 above contribute to our growth as Christians. They are actually church duties and activities, the routine of good Christians. However, in themselves they cannot make anyone good Christians, even though it is commonly understood that they do; this is simply a human belief. There must be a change from a past life to a new life.

Baptism

John indeed baptised with water, but you shall be baptised with the Holy Spirit. (Acts 11:16)

Baptism is a sign of cleaning or washing away our sin. We are dipped into water, either in church or at a bathing place, to assure us that we are now saved. Having been baptised, we become the children of God. We believe that we have been buried with Jesus Christ and raised from the dead with a new nature in the Lord. We Christians believe that baptism is very important in Christianity.

However, some of us believe that that is all, and that we can do whatever we like, simply because we have become part of the Lord's Kingdom. Truly examining the Gospel shows that is not the case.

Baptism does not make us into good Christians, nor does it even make us Christians. What makes us Christian is an acceptance of Jesus Christ as our personal Saviour. (People mistakenly call it being born again, and this will be examined later.)

The Gospel of John lets us see and understand that baptism is associated with two different things: water, and the Holy Spirit. What are these? They are not the same as each other, but they work together to fulfil one goal. In fact, it can now be seen that it is only baptism of the Holy Spirit that makes us into good Christians.

Baptism by water washes away our old sins and makes us new. From the scriptures, it can be seen that baptism is a sign of repentance and an acceptance of Jesus Christ as a personal Saviour. We repent of our sins in order to receive remission from them. It is the confession of our sins and the bad things we have done in the past, and a dedication to a new nature, a new life. It proves to others that we have become a new creation. Thus, our new life after baptism will indicate whether or not we are good Christians. Truly, it is the difference between our present and past life that counts most. It is this change that God is looking for, because this is what makes us Christians. We should realise that being baptised is an achievement. It is also vital to receive the right teaching, as well as doing the right things in accordance with the Bible, to promote the Gospel to save people's lives. It is one of the main processes enabling us to become members of God's family, and will count towards our future life.

At what stage should we be baptised, and what are churches doing about it? It is our belief that all Christians should be baptised. The question is whether the baptism should occur in the early or mature stages of our life. To baptise our children in childhood is a good thing. However, can our children know what this baptism is about? These children cannot decide on their own.

If we are baptised in the mature stage of our life, we can understand and know what this baptism is, and we can make this decision on our own. At this stage, we may know what is wrong and what is not, so we can always assess any situations personally; this can be a problem for Christians. It is important for us to be baptised in the mature stage, since this has many advantages over baptism in the earlier stage.

As we are called to worship God and to demonstrate the truth of the Gospel, it is good to consider the stage at which we are baptised, but it is not important: the most important thing is the way in which we are trained. Thus, the responsibility that we parents have is to train our children so that they are grounded in the Word of God. Many Christians are concerned about this issue, which seriously influences the Gospel and people's lives. So the stage at which we are baptised is not important, because baptism can never save us.

Types of Baptism

John answered, saying to all, "I indeed baptise you with water; but One mightier than I is coming, whose sandal strap I am not worthy to loose. He will baptise you with the Holy Spirit and fire." (Luke 3:16–17)

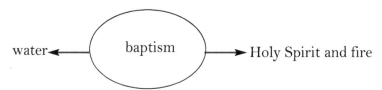

water ← baptism → Holy Spirit and fire

2.6: Types of Baptism

It may seem very strange that there are two types of baptism. *Baptism by water* is sometimes carried out by scattering drops of water on someone. It was certainly a religious rite in the Old Testament, and it is a way of baptising, especially for Christian infants. The other method of baptism by water is to dip people in water.

What is the effect of baptism on our life, and what is its importance for us? Baptism with water was a tradition still carried out in the Gospels by John the Baptist, who baptised Jesus Christ. Being baptised with water is a sign of washing away our sins, ensuring that we are saved from that moment, since we have become children of

God through acceptance of Jesus Christ as our personal Saviour. However, it is not a guarantee that we have been given everlasting life.

We can see from the above scripture that the other type of baptism is with the *Holy Spirit and fire,* and this is from Jesus Christ, and is associated with the presence of God. Any person who is baptised in this way is totally different in terms of character.

To consider these two types of baptism is to recognise that baptism in itself cannot make us Christians. The two types can be counted as step one and step two: we cannot reach step two without fulfilling step one. In fact, the two types connect, for once we have been baptised with water, it opens a way for the Holy Spirit and fire to function. We cannot become Christians without baptism of the Holy Spirit and fire.

Which baptism have we experienced?

Water baptism, and baptism with the Holy Spirit and fire

Paul said to [some disciples], "Did you receive the Holy Spirit when you believed?" So they said to him, "We have not so much as heard whether there is a Holy Spirit." And he said to them, "Into what then were you baptised?" So they said, "Into John's baptism." Then Paul said, "John indeed baptised with a baptism of repentance, saying to the people that they should believe on Him who would come after him, that is, on Christ Jesus." (Acts 19:2–4)

Water baptism is a baptism of repentance, showing that Jesus Christ came to free us from our sins by His own sacrifice. Being baptised with water is a physical matter. It lets us get ready for the Gospel, and is a preparation for receiving baptism with the Holy Spirit and fire. The preparation depends on our own will and our ability to do the work of the Gospel. This time of preparing to experience the Holy Spirit in our life may be short or long. It does not make us born-again Christians, or followers of Christ. Many of us believe in God and have been baptised, but it may seem that nothing has changed.

We may not change or maintain our good works as we do not see any profit.

The main difference between baptism by water, and baptism with the Holy Spirit and fire, is that the former is an invitation to repent of our sins; it takes place physically with water, though it is believed to have a spiritual effect. Baptism with the Holy spirit and fire comes suddenly, with no invitation; God's manifest presence and power could be experienced without any sign or warning. It occurs as a result of our willingness and commitment to do God's work, as this creates a real relationship between us and God. It is only the latter baptism that can take us to Heaven. Nobody can force us directly or indirectly to be baptised in this way; even the Lord Himself can never force us to be baptised with the Holy Spirit and fire. He has given us free will to do what we choose. It is the change in our life through doing God's work that allows us to be baptised with the Holy Spirit and fire, and continues to equip us for the Gospel of God. Being baptised with the Holy Spirit and fire is to do with spiritual matters and with authority, and is received directly from God. It enables all of us to be born again and to become one body. It enables us to speak with tongues and to prophesy.

It requires self-management, since God lets us do what we choose. At the same time, He requires purity and a commitment to move out of darkness and draw near to Him; if we are moving in a direction away from God, then we have no clue about managing our Gospel life.

This type of baptism shows us that it is God who created the world. It is to do with how we handle the Holy presence and the glory of God. It provides us with the assurance that we will see the Kingdom of God, which is yet to come. The key factor is our belief in Jesus Christ as the Son of God. This baptism is based on love, faith and willingness to do the work of God. It restores the relationship between God and His people. It acts as witness to our identification with Jesus Christ in His death and burial as well as His resurrection; it acknowledges our unfitness to be part of the Second

Coming of Christ. It joins us to Jesus Christ Himself, and is a way of examining ourselves and repenting, to glory in God's presence and power.

Communion

I received from the Lord that which I also delivered to you: that the Lord Jesus on the same night in which He was betrayed took bread; and when He had given thanks, He broke it and said, "Take, eat; this is My body which is broken for you; do this in remembrance of Me." In the same manner He also took the cup after supper, saying, "This cup is the new covenant in My blood. Do this, as often as you drink it, in remembrance of me. For as often as you eat this bread and drink this cup, you proclaim the Lord's death till He comes. (1Corinthians 11:23–26)

Communion is the act of sharing consecrated bread and wine as symbols of Christ's actual body and blood. It is a sacrament and remembrance of the death of the Lord Jesus Christ on the cross of Calvary, and His resurrection from the dead on the third day, which declares our Christian victory over the devil and everything on this earth. It is a part of our spiritual life and increases the grace of sanctification. It is normally meant for those of us who have changed from our sinful life and continue to be willing to change, so that we can continue to grow more like Christ. Those of us also who are determined to change are supposed to take communion, because the Lord placed emphasis on it. It is a demonstration of our obedience and gratefulness to God for what He has done on the cross for us.

If we take communion and yet do not change the bad things we did before we came to Christ, we cannot be genuine Christians. The scriptures assure us that before we take communion, we have to examine ourselves, in order not to take the body and the blood of the Lord while still guilty; this would bring judgement on us. As Christians, a question to ask ourselves here is: can we call ourselves born-again Christians, and continue to sin and take communion at the same time?

The Lord made it clear that communion is a remembrance of Him and the New Covenant in His blood. The New Covenant is a new agreement that God made with His people, through Jesus Christ pouring His blood out for many to forgive their sins. Jesus offered His body as a sacrifice for our sins in order to do away with sin in our life, make us alive and reconcile us to God. Jesus Christ forgave us our sins by His blood: *"Drink from it, all of you. For this is My blood of the new covenant, which is shed for many for the remission of sins." (Matthew 26:27–28)*

The Lord demonstrated to His people how we should take communion to enable us to work towards His life. He explained to us the purposes and effects of communion, so that we will be able to perform our duties under this new covenant and keep our remembrance of Him. He knew that we would not find it easy to remain in Him and in our life on earth; therefore, taking His body and blood with a sound and genuine heart is one of the main things that will enable us to remember and focus on Him all the time.

Communion is a contract between us Christians and God. God's gift of His body and blood means that He has fulfilled His side of the contract; it is now our Christian responsibility to carry out our part of the contract. Whoever wants to take communion must be aware of the terms, conditions and consequences of the contract; we have a contractual obligation to examine ourselves before taking communion. Taking communion does not make us Christians, born-again Christians or followers of Christ. Truly, we believe that communion is an act of Christian self-assessment, so that we will be able to focus on God.

Factors of communion

Therefore whoever eats this bread or drinks this cup of the Lord in an unworthy manner will be guilty of the body and blood of the Lord. But let a man examine himself, and so let him eat of the bread and drink of the cup. For he who eats and drinks in an unworthy manner eats and drinks judgment to himself, not discerning the Lord's body. For this reason many are weak and sick among you, and many sleep. (1 Corinthians 11:27–30)

Apart from the Ten Commandants, it could be said that communion (and its consequences) is the most important thing that the Lord emphasised. So in examining ourselves, we look carefully at ourselves and make some changes to the things in our life that are not good. This correction of our mistakes will keep us from sinning and doing things that are contrary to the Word of God. Truly, it is how God can know which of us are determined to work hard to worship Him. Taking communion is a responsibility that God has given to His people; it really benefits us, His children, and helps to equip us for the Gospel.

We must take time to put things in place and work towards the day or time of communion, if we really want to worship God and enjoy the Gospel. For this reason, all the members of the church must know the day of communion, so that we can examine ourselves fully before we come to church. Sometimes, we think about other people sitting near us in the church, and take communion without self-examination. Others of us take communion because if we do not, then we think that other Christians around us may say things about us or think differently of us. These things do happen in the church of God, because we do not understand the importance and consequence of communion. Before we can have communion with God, we must walk in truth. It should be impossible for us to have communion with God and not walk in His truth, but unfortunately it does happen.

There are some negative results if we not value communion and consider Jesus Christ's instructions for it. This why Paul said to the Corinthian church that the church of God is full of weak, sick and sleeping people.

Weak people: we, God's people, are not functioning as effectively as we should, both spiritually and physically. Although we proclaim that we are the children of God with the same qualities as the Lord, it seems that we lack the qualities of our God. Even in our own house or church of God we cannot prevent a mess; we sit back and let it happen, without even realising that it is our responsibility to clear it up. God will not do it for us again, since we already have the ability to perform everything.

Sick people: we are in poor health. The house of God, which is meant for prayer, is full of sick and poor people; it is now a source of woes and thieves.

Sleeping people: we are either dormant or dead. If dormant, we are not using our talents. It is a biblical truth that we are a light for the world, supposed to shine and brighten the corner where we are, for the world to see our God through us. Unfortunately, that is not the case. If dead, then we walk and worship God, and the world sees us go to church, preach the Gospel and organise crusades; however, there is nothing that is good in us and nothing good comes out of us. We do not have the Holy Spirit in us, because we take communion carelessly.

Contribution to the church

Contribution to the church is the giving of money to help a church to move on. There are two main forms: one is *conditional contribution* and the other is *unconditional contribution*.

The former is a contribution that depends on something else. The main idea behind this contribution is the intention to receive something back. We may think that our contribution to the church will open a way for us to receive more from the church than we give. There are many ways of doing this.

Some of us want to be treated as special. This does not make us Christians. This is because we want the elders of the church or the other Christians to treat us differently and to distinguish us from others on the basis of our giving. This has nothing to do with Christianity. It shows that we are still living our old life. If we are like this, it will create problems and confusion in the body of Christ, causing some Christians to backslide, as well as dealing a blow to the reputation of the Gospel.

Others of us want to create competition, trying as hard as possible to gain position or status. Truly, worshipping the Lord has nothing to do with the things of the world, neither does it deal with competition. The book of Life tells us that there should be no competition for status or gain, but that the highest ambition is to serve others in the church. However, if we let position or status rather than the Word of God become part of our lives, then we are still continuing with our old life and we cannot be considered as good Christians.

An unconditional contribution means that our gift is totally genuine, and we contribute to the church freely from our heart, to allow the Gospel to move forward. It is good for us to do this. However, if we still have our old nature (old life) and are not willing to put away the bad things, such as lying, greed and hateful feelings, and put on good things in our life, then this kind of contribution still does not in itself make us good Christians.

Evangelism

Some of us think that we are good Christians if we spread the Gospel, by advertising in the local press, magazines and newspapers, and through radio and television, inviting people to come and hear the Word of God, in order to get them to come to Christ. Also, we think that we are good Christians if we spread the Gospel news by going every week from house to house, walking from street to street, making calls daily, inviting the public to come and hear the best singers in the church. However, again, this does not make us good Christians, if we have not yet turned away from the bad things we were doing before we accepted the Lord as our personal Saviour. If we do not refrain from this rebellion and ask the Lord for forgiveness, then we have not yet become Christians, even though we have been baptised.

Going to church

Then if anyone says to you, "Look, here is the Christ!" or "There!" do not believe it. For false Christs and false prophets will rise and show great signs and wonders to deceive, if possible, even the elect. (Matthew 24:23–4)

Going to church is very important for our Christian life. The main purpose of going to church is to worship God with other Christians, to show our love and appreciation to God, and to have fellowship with others. The church is God's present instrument through which He desires to extend His Kingdom and fulfil His purpose. We want to worship God, to walk in the Lord's footsteps and to learn other parts of Christian doctrine (teaching) to assist and equip us to promote the Gospel, not to show off our worldly goods, such as achievements, clothes and property.

If we go to church without refraining from the bad things that we have done in the past, or even being willing to leave them, then we are not yet new creatures, because nothing has changed in our life. Not all Christians in the church of God are followers of Christ. So, going to church in itself does not make us into good and genuine Christians, as many people think.

Following Christ's teachings

Then Jesus said to those Jews who believed Him, "If you abide in my word, you are My disciples indeed. And you shall know the truth, and the truth shall make you free." (John 8:31–2)

Jesus Christ taught His disciples to follow Him by doing the things that He was doing. The Lord told them that it was only through doing what He was doing that they would follow Him. So, if we have decided to follow the Lord, then we ought to do the things that please Him. It is a biblical truth that by doing what the Lord desires and by following His teachings, we can become true Christians. Some of us put ourselves in the position of Jesus Christ and tell others to do the work of God, while we ourselves do not bother to do it. If we do the same things that Jesus Christ taught His disciples to do, but are not really involved in the practical aspects of Christ's teachings, this does not make us Christians. It might prove our Christianity to others, rather than allowing them to become Christians.

Offerings and paying tithes

And He [Jesus] looked up and saw the rich putting their gifts into the treasury, and He saw also a certain poor widow putting in two mites. So He said, "Truly I say to you that this poor widow has put in more than all; for all these out of their abundance have put in offerings for God, but she out of her poverty put in all the livelihood that she had." (Luke 21:1–4)

Tithe is paying one tenth of one's goods or income for the support of a church. *"Bring all the tithes into the storehouse, that there may be food in My house, and try Me now in this," says the Lord of hosts, "If I will not open for you the windows of heaven, and pour out for you such blessing, that there will not be room enough to receive it." (Malachi 3:10)*

Tithe funds are used for God's purposes such as to build and maintain churches, and to carry on the work of God.

We do not become Christians by giving offerings of money, nor by paying tithes to God's ministry. The offerings and the tithes that we pay are to support the church and help it move on, to assist needy Christians and those who are suffering in the body of Christ (the church). Also, this money will assist members of the public who are in need, to improve their situation and to show that God loves and cares for them.

Truly, it is very good for us to do this. However, giving offerings, paying tithes to the church or giving money to others do not save our life; they demonstrate that we love and thank God, and that we show love for what He has done for us. We could do all these good things and inwardly we may be still doing things that belong to our old nature; being in our old life before we came to Christ cannot save us because we are still in darkness.

It is necessary to focus on the Word of God more than anything else, since God is not looking for our ability to donate to His Kingdom. Instead, He is looking for us, His children, who fear Him and obey His Commandments, and with commitment in our hearts are working towards the Gospel goal.

Prayer and fasting

Prayer is the act of speaking or offering worship to God. It is a conversation and intercession with God to forgive our sin. It is the master key for forgiveness, peace, help and breakthrough. It also enables us to forgive our sisters' and brothers' sins against us. Therefore, by praying to God with faith, we can overcome every difficult situation and let us acknowledge a breakthrough, in order to fulfil our mission with the help of the Holy Spirit.

Every prayer includes a response. So, when we pray to God, He has to respond to our prayer. This response from God is very important, because it shows the presence of God and our relationship with Him. Also, it demonstrates God's love and care for us. God's response assures us one way or another of the outcome of our prayer, and makes that particular prayer meaningful. Therefore, prayer to God without feedback from God can be seen as useless.

Many of us pray to God constantly for our needs, but unfortunately do not think that there should be any response from God; we do not even bother to think about the failure of God's response. His response to our prayer is not that He has to provide us with what we have prayed for at that particular moment. Instead, it is more something to do with the presence of God at the moment of prayer. This presence makes that thing successful, and it gives peace to us when we pray. This is especially important when we feel empty. Our emptiness can only be filled by God's presence in our life. His presence assures and encourages us that our prayer has been heard and that God will deal with it. If this happens, we are comforted and strengthened, no matter what the circumstances of our prayer.

Prayer is essential in our life. Praying to God will enable us to grow, both spiritually and physically. It will allow us to overcome our problems and focus on God's work rather than focusing on worldly matters.

Fasting involves taking no food or little food, while praying to God about a particular matter. It is biblical, so all of us are entitled to do it, but there is no obligation for us to fast. However, it can contribute to our growth and open a way for us to achieve something. We can do it on any day, taking in no food from morning onwards. We can fast from three to seven days without even a drop of water.

Prayer and fasting work together to provide one result and function in accordance with the Word of God. The purpose and outcome of this depends on what we are looking for or what we want God to do for us. It is one of the vital aspects of our Christian life, because it builds our relationship with God, and helps us to correct mistakes, rid ourselves of unhealthy things and focus on the Word of God. Only He can answer prayer and fasting. The outcome will not just happen, but depends on whether we are willing to do our Christian work. Many of us now do much fasting and prayer, with the aim of receiving the result, because we are Christians. Prayer and fasting do not make us Christians, but they help us to grow. We are not entitled to receive our requests from our prayer and fasting, since we might pray and fast all the time, but are not willing to change our lives. Many of us are in this situation, doing the same thing all the time. We are 'playing fast and loose', doing one thing in church and another thing at home, with a double identity.

Reading and learning from the Bible and religious books

Reading the Bible and Christian books helps us understand the life of Christ and His teachings more, and know what is right to do. Also, it guides us, and prevents us from doing wrong things as we did in the past before we came to Christ. It helps us find out how to become good Christians and how to live our life as pleases God. This enables us to build and strengthen our faith in God and experience the glory of the Lord and the Gospel blessings. It has nothing to do with making us Christians, or good Christians. Many of us today teach, read and learn from the Bible and religious books, while we still live as we did before we became Christians.

Good Christians and Bad Christians

But the hour is coming, and now is, when the true worshippers will worship the Father in spirit and truth: for the Father is seeking such to worship Him. (John 4:23)

This scripture carefully indicates that the people of God will worship Him either truly or falsely. There are two main types – *good Christians and bad Christians.*

What type of Christian we are in the ministry of God depends on our own agenda, which means what we want to do. Unfortunately, most of us in the body of Christ come with different motives. We come to Christ's ministry with our own agendas, rather than the agenda of worshipping God. Every successful person has an agenda, which helps us move forward always, to work towards and fulfil our vision. It can be described as a tool of success. It is very important for all of us in Christ's ministry to be aware of our agenda. It is our character or behaviour that shows what type of Christians we are. There are many different people in the Body of Christ and we all call ourselves true Christians, letting those who come into the body of Christ call themselves Christians. As far as the human point of view is concerned, we are all true Christians. However, it is not what we do in church that makes us into true Christians. God, whom we worship, sees people totally differently. Good Christians are those of us who are committed to the Word of God, enabling us to become Christ's followers. We sincerely do the will of God after accepting Jesus Christ as our personal Saviour through baptism. This classifies us as true Christians because we always try to do the will of God. We always seek to be lowly and humble. True Christian nature can be described in terms of the life of Christ. If we feed on the right type of food, it will enable us to grow like Christ. This right type of food is not actual food that we normally eat at home to sustain our life and growth, but refers to the Word of God. Good Christians are aware of the consequences of bad behaviour and know that adopting bad behaviour is adverse to our growth. We understand that being good Christians is war. It is war because it is not easy in this world to have the genuine ambition to fulfil the Gospel mission and to do God's work. Being good Christians as a result of doing God's work will mean trouble for us. However, we always try to dispose of our sin, since we know that it will let us empty ourselves, so that we can work towards a life with God. We understand that hardship is part of life, and that before we can accomplish our Gospel mission and be successful in life, we have to go through hardship. It is only hardship that can prepare us to meet the adversities of life.

We understand that we need some of the world's goods in order to sustain our life on this planet. However, we do not depend on them, since we know that everybody is committed to death and the grave, and that whatever we have will be left behind when we die. We are more interested in applying the Word of God in our life. We seriously try to commit ourselves to the Gospel and to keep our promise to our Gospel responsibilities. We definitely know the benefits of the Gospel, and are inwardly determined to follow in the footsteps of Christ and study the Bible at every moment. Spiritual growth leads us to be mature Christians; this does not mean that we have grown up, but refers to an understanding of the Word of God and its application, resulting in wisdom.

Bad Christians do not have a firm and deep grounding in the Word of God as a priority. Anything can disturb them and easily move them away from the Kingdom of God. Although they care about the Gospel, they do not seriously focus on God. They are interested in studying the Word of God but find it difficult to apply. They prepare themselves to receive the Lord, but in one way or another cannot adopt the Christian life. They are aware that unworthy things cannot do them good, but cannot get rid of them. One outstanding thing about bad Christians is that they cannot abandon the complexity of city life.

Bad Christians can also be considered as Anti-Christ, who have come into the Kingdom of God with a different mission. Many people in the church are Anti-Christ, doing the work of Satan instead of God. It is naïve of them not to study and equip themselves with the Word of God. Many Christians destroy others because they lack the understanding and application of the Word of God. It is difficult to spot them; doing so is the work of the Holy Spirit.

The Kingdom of God (God's church) experiences many problems which are beyond understanding. As Christians, we think about all that is happening in our local church, and ask ourselves why this is so. Whether bad Christians are seen as true Christians or Anti-Christian usually depends upon their Christian ambition. If we are Christians, then it is our duty and responsibility to believe God and His Word, study and learn from it, and put it into practice, to equip ourselves for the Gospel. An Anti-Christian does the same thing for God's people, believing that they are Spirit-filled Christians, so that they can confuse or convince the people of God one way or another, to fulfil their own ambition.

Born Again

Jesus Christ answered [Nicodemus], "Most assuredly, I say to you, unless one is born of water and the Spirit, he cannot enter the kingdom of God." (John 3:5)

Born again means to be born of water and Spirit indicating that we are washed with water and spirit. This enables us to receive forgiveness for our sin, and a cure for the causes of our sin and disease, in order to make us new. There are many differences between baptism and being born again. When we are baptised, we are nearly, but not yet, the property of God. We still have some distance ahead of us to accomplish. This distance can be short or long, depending on our application of the Word of God and our actual life on this planet. When we are born again, we are constantly aware of the Holy Spirit's presence, and we can bear witness to God. A born-again person is God's property, and so we are totally bound to do God's will and to follow His Word. We demonstrate that we are walking in newness of life after baptism; we constantly walk in love, light and wisdom, and we find out what is acceptable to God rather than to humans. In fact, born-again people experience the presence and glory of the Holy Spirit in our life, like those who experienced the same thing on the day of Pentecost. We are flexible, and allow the Holy Spirit to transform us, because we are determined to fulfil our Gospel tasks and wish to receive the peace of God before we die.

Born of flesh, water and spirit

There are three forms of birth: we are born of flesh, born of water and born of spirit. The word flesh here means sin, so being born of flesh refers to someone who is considered to be born in sin. Since it comes with human birth, all humans inherit this kind of sin. Our ancestors were Adam and Eve, who sinned against

God, so we have all sinned against God as well. Adam and Eve's sin has become an inheritance of our generation, so it is our human responsibility to do something about it. Being born of water is used as evidence of our new beginning, indicating that we have had a new birth, so we have set aside our flesh. Water is vital to human life, because it is something that gives and sustains life. This water is sometimes seen as the water of life, so being born of water is symbolic of our new life. If we are born of water, then this water has washed away the sins that we have confessed; we have received a new life, as well as the fact that we are doing the will of God. Being born of the spirit refers to the baptism by the Holy Spirit, which is totally different from being born of water. Our spiritual life is maintained, for we have been renewed in our spirit. This kind of Spirit can be seen at the Day of Pentecost.

Pentecost is the Greek name for a festival, celebrated at the end of the grain harvest, known in the Old Testament as the Feast of Weeks (Leviticus 23:15). The Day of Pentecost was early on after the resurrection of Jesus Christ, narrated in the book of Acts. Many disciples experienced a miraculous speaking in foreign tongues, which enabled people with different languages to understand their message. Thus, the disciples witnessed the birth of the New Testament church and the Holy Spirit dwelling in all believers. All of us who have been through this baptism of the Holy Spirit have this; however, it is our responsibility to experience its presence. The Holy Spirit is always with us as He was on the Day of Pentecost, and we can be constantly aware of the Holy Spirit's presence.

Differences between True and False Christians

The aim of *true* Christians is to do away with the sins that no one knows and the sins that everyone knows, and to concentrate on God's Word. We want our life to be illuminated by the presence of the Lord, to enable us to seek the lost so that they might be saved and redeemed. We always look forward to the Lord's coming, and try to prepare ourselves for the Lord to come at any time. We constantly aim to gain our everlasting life, and because of this, we always try to devote ourselves to God, and are committed and determined to obey God's Word.

False Christians do not turn away from their sins. They aim to create many problems in the body of Christ, to destroy the Gospel, and to prevent us obtaining peace on this Earth and in our everlasting life. They act as agents for Satan, for him to obtain some people for his kingdom.

False Christians come into the body of Christ to destroy God's work. They study the Word of God to equip themselves to accomplish their mission. They know the Bible deeply, taking time to study it, to enable them to avoid problems or criticism from us. They come to church and study the Bible in the same way as us. However, they have a different purpose. They are interested in false teaching and misrepresentation of the Gospel. Their preaching is based on worldly goods, and they focus on teaching about prosperity, since they are much more interested in this. Their priority is to acquire property and worldly goods, rather than to deliver the good news to save people's lives; they know that in this way they can influence us to come to their kingdom, which is hell, and destroy us.

Characteristics of True and Good Christians

Characteristics are the manner in which we feel something and act on it. Our characteristics determine whether we are good or bad. Our character is vital because it can influence the lives of others. Apart from the Lord, nobody knows what will take our life on this earth, but our character might lead us to die in a shorter time.

If people have bad characteristics, this refers to the wrong things that they feel and do in their lives. Here are some of the examples of bad characteristics: taking drugs, stealing, envy, and sexual immorality. Some people think that practising these behaviours will allow them to succeed in life and achieve their personal purpose. This lifestyle choice does affect their chances of long life, and increases the risk of failing in life and dying prematurely.

Many people die every day. As Christians, have we asked ourselves the reasons for this? It is our belief that the majority of people die because of bad characteristics. In this twenty-first century, many people have died from AIDS, and every day people are still dying from it around the world. At the same time, the number of people who are infected by HIV (AIDS) is constantly rising every minute. It has come to the point that something needs to be done to put a stop to this crisis and for someone to take the initiative. When we look at the problem carefully, it is not a matter of having the right medicine to cure AIDS, nor is it the money to buy medicine that can solve the problem. Surely, the main solution to the problem is to deal with character. It is the people themselves who have to deal with their bad characteristics and get rid of them, because they are infecting others as a result of sexual immorality and drug-taking.

Good characteristics increase the chance of success in life and reduce the chances of dying prematurely. Any lifestyle choices brought about by good characteristics can lead us to a long life.

Our Christian characteristics are the ways in which we should behave, in order to distinguish us from others. They indicate whether or not we are devoted to worshipping God. We have a fundamental belief in the religious principles of right and wrong; this is a feature of Christianity and makes us true followers of Christ. Adhering to this will lead us to a life of joy and peace, and will lead us home. It will let us experience new things coming into our life, and this will encourage us to do more to become like the Master himself.

Some of us let worldly things block the joy of our salvation; we let worldly pressures take away our blessings all the time. We do this instead of adopting genuine characteristics, to demonstrate that we belong to one God through the second birth that is our inheritance from Jesus Christ. It is this Christian characteristic that distinguishes us from others.

One thing that troubles us is that we have no idea about what will help our growth. We may show good characteristics and feel much better when we come to church. Yet at home, we are totally different, and people around us are dying because of our character or attitude. Some of us always pretend to be good, seeming to be like angels, while inwardly we are not. This brings a question for us to answer: if we are Christians, how many times have we ignored wrong things occurring at church or in church work, things that destroy God's ministry now or in the future? Is it good to step in to express our concern, or to stay back?

Before we become Christians, we have to be real and genuine. This is what God is looking for, because it is through us that others can become true Christians and do God's work. The Bible emphasises that we cannot be false Christians and still do the work of God. To be false Christians implies that we are worshipping two gods, and are willing to do good and bad things. Nobody is perfect, and at times we do bad things. However, if we are willing to do bad things, we cannot become members of Christ's ministry, because we do not want to change from our past behaviour. Changing from past things to present things is the new life shown in the Bible.

Many Christians are in bondage to other Christians in God's ministry, because of these bad characteristics. We are bond-Christians, to other Christians instead of to God. They do not let freedom reign in the body of Christ, which is an important step on the road to promoting the Gospel. There are harsh conditions in the ministry of God, because of others' attitudes. They do not allow us to focus on God, to enable us to grow and to do our mission work. If this issue is not dealt with and the situation arrested, we will lose patience, and this will cause us more problems. All these problems caused by people's bad characteristics are because of lack of training. God's ministries should train people to produce enough real and genuine pastors and teachers, to preach and teach the valuable Bible message to God's people, and help us focus on God. In this way, people's bad characteristics and attitudes will not take us away from the body of Christ. Before we can grow and become true Christians, we need to receive the true Bible message, to enable us to change and move our mind away from the bad characteristics we had before we came to God.

Therefore, as the elect of God, holy and beloved, put on tender mercies, kindness, humility, meekness, long suffering; bearing with one another, and forgiving one another, if anyone has a complaint against another; even as Christ forgave you, so you also must do. But above all these things put on love, which is the bond of perfection. (*Colossians 3:12–14*)

True Christians have the following characteristics: Bearing with one another

Bearing with one another means supporting or holding someone; it is connecting and linking with each other, acting as support for everyone. All of us are one body and have one goal, which is to proclaim the Gospel to save people's lives. Without bearing with one another, it would be impossible to achieve this goal. The goal was assigned to all Christians by the Lord Jesus Christ to accomplish before His Second Coming. Knowing the difficulties involved in this task, He has given us tools to overcome the problems. So we must do our best to make use of these tools, such as bearing with one another, because there is no other way for us to fulfil the goal.

Bearing with one another is not easy for us human beings, even though we are Christians. It can be successful if we really know our objectives and have a deep understanding of our Lord's Gospel teachings as well as their outcomes. It is totally based on love, and it is this love that we are lacking. It is necessary to ask ourselves how we are going to achieve this task. We let all the vain things on this earth charm us more than anything else. This means that we have no love and we do not trust each other. It has wiped out our love for each other, which is one of the paramount parts of Christian doctrine.

Forgiveness

This is the act of giving up our wish to punish or take revenge. It is usually based on repentance and the willingness to make restitution. It concerns willingly letting go of someone's mistake or fault, without having hard feelings towards them. Some mistakes or sins can be easily forgiven; others can be forgiven, but still we have hard feelings towards the people when we remember and think about them. The Lord asks us to willingly forgive all kinds of mistakes and sins. He asks us to totally forgive anyone who sins against us, as He always forgives us our sins. He continues to say that it is a sin not to forgive and forget, if someone sins against us; if we do not forgive, then we do not love the Lord. We cannot love God and hate our brothers and sisters who sin against us. Doing that would mean that we are liars and, as a result, we will not live. The Lord knows that forgiveness has a real purpose for our life in this world, and this emphasis shows us its importance in the Gospel. If we do not adopt this characteristic of forgiveness, it is hard to become true Christians.

Humility

Humility is having a realistic sense of what we are before God and other people, being honest before God and thinking in lowly terms of ourselves. Humbling ourselves could be costly in some ways, such as in our societies or communities. However, the consequence of such an attitude of humility may give us some credit, since God takes pleasure in our efforts to humble ourselves and loves to bless and exalt the humble ones.

In the book of Philippians, Paul wrote about Jesus Christ: *He humbled Himself and became obedient to the point of death, even the death of the cross. Therefore God also highly exalted Him and given Him the name which is above every name, that at the name of Jesus every knee should bow, of those in heaven, and of those on earth, and of those under the earth, and that every tongue should confess that Jesus Christ is Lord, to the glory of God, the Father. (Philippians 2:8–11)*

Humility demonstrates our human spirit and proves what we are. It is our duty to adopt this characteristic and exercise it to everybody, as Jesus Christ did. If we show humbleness of mind only to God without doing it to our brothers and sisters, then our Christianity is totally in vain. We need to accept all human beings as brothers and sisters.

Longsuffering

This means accepting with patience any pain, injury or trouble that we may experience. It can also mean waiting for a breakthrough, an achievement, or for something good to happen. It is one of the key characteristics for us to fulfil our Gospel mission. It is one of the most important roots of the Gospel achieved by the Lord Jesus Christ. Without this, our lives would also not be saved.

However, many so-called followers of Christ do not even want to know about it. It is amazing that we have decided to follow in our Master's footsteps, and yet not want to experience this longsuffering, in order to wait for important things to come to pass, and to experience the blessings of salvation. It is because we are dealing with worldly things.

It is very sad that we cannot see that it is this longsuffering that enabled the Lord Jesus Christ to accomplish His vision for us. We can now boldly speak out that we are conquerors of the world. As His followers, we are supposed to be longsuffering, to be well grounded in the Word of God, which will enable us to be outstanding. This will equip us to stand firm against the forces of the world, to fulfil the task that the Lord has given to us.

Some of us do not want any delay in anything. If we have asked for something from God, and there is a delay, we may think that God has denied it; therefore, we quickly become frustrated or disappointed, and as a result we give up. A delay does not necessarily mean that it will not come to pass, or that the Lord, who created us and knows us better than we do, has denied our request.

Love

This means a kindly influence, loving-kindness, and sensitivity to and a respect for the dignity and the needs of other people. It is the most important thing in the Gospel, because it is through this love that the Lord Jesus Christ came to save His children. It is the main root of the doctrine of Christ and has opened up the way for the lives of all people to be saved. Wherever the Lord went, He emphasised love, to let people of God know its importance to the Gospel and to humankind. It is so valuable that even money cannot buy it. The Lord knows its value both for the Gospel and for people, and encourages us to show love. Jesus Christ knows that if we adopt this love we will experience its fruits, which are patience, forgiveness, obedience, humility and respect, and that lead us to fulfil His mission of saving His children.

Kindness

Kindness is doing a good thing to another person instead of harm. Kindness must be our attitude, and doing good things must come from the heart. Our attitude should be genuine, so that we will be totally different from the people around us. We should be kind one to each other and to all human beings. We need to try to assist people; this may make us happy or unhappy, but we can always experience the joy of our salvation. As followers of Christ, we must be open and gracious so that people can always approach us, especially people who may think that they have nobody to care for them because of their low position or because they feel useless.

Meekness

Meekness is the act of yielding to someone's actions, which may be the authority or control by someone else or by a group. Meekness is a type of humble obedience. It is not easy for us to take on this characteristic. In the Bible, even Moses, who was considered as the meekest of people, was sometimes wrathful. However, the Bible encourages us in this meekness, for otherwise our Christian actions will be in vain. Therefore, meekness is necessary in our Christian life and in the Gospel of Christ.

Tender mercies

This is compassion or sympathy for other people, especially those who have problems or are suffering. Tender mercies are something concrete that we can do to show love and care for other people of God. People may be in pain, injured in an accident, hungry or offended. Having tender mercies for others acts as a symbol of family, because we feel that we belong to a family or that we have a family who love and care about us. This makes us very proud and in another way helps get rid of our pain or trouble.

We should copy these characteristics of Christ, to lead us to the

Gospel work and fulfil our ambition. Doing this will, in turn, influence our life and that of the people around us. It will demonstrate Christ's life and give an understanding of Christian faith that will lead the public to recognise God and be part of His ministry.

Characteristics of False Christians

Now the works of the flesh are evident, which are: adultery, fornication, uncleanness, lewdness, idolatry, sorcery, hatred, contentions, jealousies, outbursts of wrath, selfish ambitions, dissensions, heresies, envy, murders, drunkenness, revelries, and the like; of which I tell you beforehand, just as I also told you in time past, that those who practise such things will not inherit the kingdom of God. (Galatians 5:19–21)

This shows us the typical characteristics of people who walk in the flesh, people who cannot be classified as followers of God. These characteristics are the opposite of born-again Christians. Anything that is involved in the flesh deals with Satan.

False Christians do not humble themselves, they are always interested in miracles, and they preach about unworthy goods. They fight for position and personal interest in the Church, even though immature Christians also, at times, do the same things.

They use the name of God to cheat, steal and do all sorts of bad things, in order to discourage true Christians from worshipping God. They intentionally undermine the Gospel and fail to teach the true Gospel, in order to set the people of God in the bondage of Satan. They always want to get people into harsh conditions, and are determined to mislead people. They are very interested in dictatorship, so that others cannot express their views on important matters; they understand that people's collective views or experiences have a huge impact on others' lives. Again, they know that sharing with other people definitely builds bridges between them. They always defend their decision to do wrong things, rather than accepting and refraining from these actions. They are not learners of God, and do not seek lost people who might be saved and redeemed from their sins.

Importance of Christians

This is the way in which Christians should be treated in the Christian ministry or in the body of Christ. It is worrying to see that some Christians are not recognised as valuable people with special qualities.

What is *quality* and what is a special quality? Quality is something that makes someone or something different from others. Our quality distinguishes us and shows us to be outstanding. With the people of God, it refers to our natural gift, and is something that God gives to His people. All the children of God have this kind of quality, but how we use this quality is totally different from how others use it.

Special qualities can be described as exceptional natural gifts given by God to His people. They classify all of the children of God and human beings as the same, regardless of nationality, gender and position. We are human beings who are born to die and be buried, and nobody is more important than others, although we may be different from others in character. This gift of special qualities is based on the equal valuation of every child of God.

It is hard to understand this issue of treating some Christians differently. In the eyes of the Lord, everybody is important and precious. The Lord knows and sees Christians as very special, because we are the inheritors of His Kingdom in the future. The Lord created all of us in His image, therefore all of us have knowledge, wisdom and the talent to think, take decisions and do things. Any change in circumstances or fortune does not imply that we are finished or useless. If we use our position in the church or our talents to treat others differently, it is as if we are God or are perfect like Christ. However, we are all in Christ's ministry to learn how to live the life of Christ and to copy His character, as well as to study and exercise His Gospel. Why are we doing this? Some of us do this to make others have confidence in us and this probably gives us a huge boost. We do all sorts of things for fame, and we influence others to depend on us always to make decisions. Truly, we do this for human merit, in order to get members into what we call 'our churches', or we convince people to follow us in other ways, to achieve our personal purposes. (The phrase 'our churches' means that some Christians claim the ownership of the Lord's churches. This issue will be discussed later.)

We are in the ministry of Christ to learn and study from each other, to express our views and to correct our mistakes, in order to grow into true Christians, enabling us to do the work of God to His expectations. Being Christians does not mean that we are not allowed to express our views about church matters, or that we must be the followers of just certain people or group of people, or be brainwashed by others. These problems, especially brainwashing, cause serious damage to both Christianity and to us ourselves.

Brainwashing means intentionally, directly or indirectly forcing others gradually or convincing them to side with us always, so that they will not voice their own ideas and beliefs. When people are brainwashed, they are willing to accept any decision, no matter what the outcome. The outcome of any decision is essential, because it shows the fruit of the decision; whether the fruit is good or bad, it always has an impact.

Here is an example of brainwashing. It is a known phenomenon that we, the people of God, should not have a say in church matters or the leaders of the church, such as pastors and elders, since they are the servants of God and have been chosen by God to lead His people. Therefore, if people express any view about church matters led by these pastors or elders, then it is a curse. On the other hand, God will destroy us because we do not have the right to disagree with God's chosen servants or make any comments on their actions.

This is not right, because the Gospel is like a democracy, in which we do have the right to express our views about the Gospel and matters that concern the church. Everybody should be treated equally, regardless of position or talent. This situation is further confused daily, since the issue about how to treat Christians is usually made by other Christians in the same body. The failure to value some Christians is a result of not respecting us and allowing us to express our views. It is then very hard to defend the Gospel, Christianity or the Christian church and its purpose.

The church is our home and is a place where we all belong. The church belongs to us, and also belongs to God, so no human beings have the authority to take control or destroy us, God's people, in our own home. It is our environment, even if we are evil, if we misbehave or do wrong. We are benefactors to other human beings, and we should have the desire to promote the happiness of the people of God. We cannot do this unless we do what we should. If we do, it will do Christianity the world of good, and will let us have some credibility in society and our community. Happiness does not just mean giving money to help others, but also doing something good to relieve the hardship of other people; this includes listening to their concerns, discussing matters with them, and finding solutions to their problems.

There is a strong belief that those Christians who do not let us express our views or concerns about the ministry of Christ do this to scare us genuine Christians who really want to worship God, and try to shut our mouths. They do this, not to do God's people or the ministry any good, but to allow them to use God's name or property for their own personal purpose. What we should bear in mind is that if we are not allowed to express our views, or people refuse to listen to our concerns, what will happen sooner or later? We will find out that our fellow Christians have misused us, or have tried to achieve their own ambitions rather than the ambition of the Gospel.

It is well known that we become Christians for a purpose. We go to church for a purpose, to worship God and nothing else. We worship God hoping that good news will come out of this, God willing. Therefore, if something goes wrong in the church, this might stop us worshipping God. We have the right to express our views about some matter, in order to put things right. Expressing our views or concerns does not imply that we are against God's work, or that we are evil.

God has chosen us for a purpose and we cannot fulfil this purpose without developing spiritually and physically. In order to develop and fulfil God's purpose for His people, He has given us all knowledge and wisdom. It is up to us to make use of this, to enable our growth in many ways, so that we can glorify God's name. Since this growth depends on us ourselves, we have to use our knowledge and wisdom to sort out good from bad, and to avoid others who want to destroy our Christianity.

The Bible states truly that there may be many false Christians who come to God's Kingdom for different purposes. These people are not doing what they are supposed to do. They do not come to God's Kingdom for nothing, but rather for a purpose. They use all sorts of tricks to influence us, so they may achieve their aims. Through being naïve and hypocritical Christians, lacking a deep understanding of God's Word, some Christians are making the worship of God very difficult for others and even for themselves.

This has a serious impact on our lives, since it does not bring us closer to God. Measures are urgently needed to get rid of these burdens on God's people and to bring all these crises to an end, because the longer they last, the greater the damage will be. It is our Christian responsibility to deal with such problems, since we are the ones who are suffering. We should be able to fulfil our calling in the Christian ministry, to thank God for choosing us and seeing us as essential, instead of fulfilling any human purpose that will end in a mess.

Christianity is about following in the footsteps of Jesus Christ, to do the right thing and to put things right. As Christians, we should be very happy to be in the ministry of Christ and willing to work to save people's lives. This contribution is important and is what Christianity is about. We must be aware that doing God's work is difficult, yet God wants to see us through all sorts of difficulties, problems and forces of this earth. In spite of the adversities that He may acquaint us with, we should be happy always, because we are very important and God has chosen us to do His work. We will be even happier when we do our Christian work faithfully and see the Lord Jesus Christ.

Basic Elements of the Gospel

And of His fullness we have all received, and grace for grace. For the law was given through Moses, but grace and truth came through Jesus Christ. (John1:16–17)

An element is anything that makes up something. It is very important because it is one of many parts on which something depends, and cannot be separated or taken away. This element is something on which someone is dependent. Relying on something or someone is essential, since we are in trouble if the thing or person is not there.

The basic elements of the Gospel are things that make up the Christian Gospel. It is essential for us to know what the Gospel consists of, because it shows us the reasons why we are Christians and our responsibilities. It also allows us to assess ourselves, to empty ourselves through our own will, and to do the Gospel work without depending on other people. We are aware that our Christian success does not depend on anybody but ourselves.

Though we may depend on someone for support or help, our success depends on our will and commitment. Every promotion in Christ's ministry is usually dependent on our commitment and our consistent hard work. Promotion here is not our position or post in the church or the body of Christ. It is our experience of the Word of God through Gospel benefits and tokens, resulting from keeping our promise to our responsibilities. It is amazing that most of us think that our success depends on other Christians, and so we rely on them for success. We do not know that even God who created us and cares for us always is not responsible for doing our work for us, especially Gospel work.

There are two main elements of the Gospel or Christianity, namely, the Word of God (the Bible) and Christians. The Bible consists of the New Testament and the Old Testament. It is believed to be written by God through His people, in their languages, which are Hebrew, Aramaic and Greek. It is accepted as God's only Words. People who want to worship God have to accept and worship Jesus Christ as the Lord, and accept the content of this holy book. The most outstanding benefits of this Bible are the Ten Commandments, grace, and the glory that was received through Moses and Jesus Christ. (John 1:17)

Christian Mission Hindrance

Christian mission is the special work assigned by God to all Christians. We should go into other places and parts of the world to spread our belief, which is the Gospel, to save the lives of God's people. We cannot tackle this work without developing and growing in faith in God, since this will provide us with the confidence to work for God, allowing us to go out there to spread our belief.

Christian mission hindrance means the factors that hold back our progress in continuing to fulfil our religious task. These factors have an increasing influence on everyday Christian life, like the influence of growth hormone. The factors regulate our growth, allowing us to grow out of bad habits and to adopt the habits of Christ, which gives us the authority and power to do God's work. These factors affect our life, both spiritually and physically. Our success depends on our focus on these factors. On the other hand, failure to consider them makes us unready for the Gospel task of spreading Christian belief in all parts of the world and to convert people to Christianity; this is known as missionary work. Doing God's work puts us on track to achieve our goal.

There are things that need to be overcome before we can fulfil our Gospel ambition. As Christians, we have to gain something from the Gospel, and this can be successful only if we undertake and obey our duties and responsibilities. These things are the orders from the Lord to His followers. Failure to obey will hinder us from experiencing the Gospel blessings.

The Bible states truly that there will be showers of blessings if we trust and obey God. Trust and obedience are not just spiritual, but also practical. Trust is having faith in God and relying on Him that, in every situation, no matter what happens, the Lord will never forget or forsake us. It is having no doubt that God will prevail. Doubt is one of our biggest problems, causing downfall, and dragging us away from following Christ. We all have this problem, and cannot get it out of our minds. We doubt especially when things are go wrong or weigh us down. In this Bible, this kind of doubt was the disciples' problem. The main example of this is Thomas, who wanted to see things with his own eyes before he could trust. He said to Jesus after the resurrection, My Lord and my God! (John 20:28), and he has become a well-known disciple because of this. At times, doubt can help, but it is a big problem influencing Christian development.

There are other problems hindering our Christian mission: Lack of understanding of God's Word

This is when we lack knowledge of the Gospel and the teachings of the Lord Jesus Christ. Many people are becoming Christians these days, and put in the work necessary to become good Christians. However, they lack deep understanding of the Word of God and Christ's teachings. From the highest to the lowest rank of Christians, these problems exist, and something needs to be done to arrest the situation. Failure to understand God's Word blocks our development and our experience of its manifestation.

This occurs as a result of spiritual and practical aspects. Again, God's Word deals with these two factors. The Holy Spirit and we Christians ourselves are the factors of Christian success in Gospel work. As far as the teachings of Jesus Christ are concerned, the Holy Spirit has to work together with us to obtain good results from God's Word. As partners, we have our own part to play and responsibility to fulfil. Failure to perform can cause a failed outcome.

The spiritual aspect deals with spiritual matters which are part of the Gospel, and are the work of the Holy Spirit. The Holy Spirit is the Spirit of God, acting for God and interacting between God and Christians. He gives spiritual gifts to us, to equip us for God's ministry. Just as the Holy Spirit has His part to play in the Gospel, so do we; He is obliged to perform only His work, and not what we are supposed to do. He cannot leave His work and do ours. The Holy Spirit has nothing to do with physical work; this is our responsibility. So, in any physical matter, there is no question of asking the Holy Spirit. It is up to us to intervene in such matters and to take action, by applying the Word of God practically, instead of expecting the Holy Spirit to do our work for us.

The practical aspect needs us to be willing to do something, without someone else's, influence, initiative or effort. We often expect the Holy Spirit to do our work for us, without knowing that the Holy Spirit has His own responsibilities and we have our own responsibilities. This physical aspect concerns the application of the Word of God. So as Christians, we must deal with physical things, by putting God's Word into practice and also speaking about situations that we believe are good for God's ministry or church.

If we believe that Christianity depends on human beings or practical things, then people will depend on us for God's worship. We need to depend on the Word of God and fulfil our Christian ability and our commitment.

We Christians ourselves

We are people who have repented of our sin and turned from it, with a desire to make restoration by living a new life, the life of God. This means that we have rid ourselves of our bad characteristics and put on a good character. We are responsible for all aspects of Christ's work within His ministry. We are to be blamed for our lack of development because of our bad character.

This contributes to the hindrance of our mission. We have a part to play in our life and Christ's ministry, in order to let the Holy Spirit assist our growth. Most of us think that as long as we are followers of Christ, we do not need to work or study, because these are things of the world. Others of us think that God always takes care of us and is in control of our needs; therefore, we do not need to worry about what we will eat or drink, because almighty God will definitely provide us with whatever we want. Of course, the Bible states that God takes care of His children and provides for our needs. However, it does not imply that we can sit down and fold our arms. If we are healthy and strong, it is our responsibility to perspire in order to earn our daily bread, and also to provide it for those around us who do not have the chance because of sickness or problems. God is in control of us and takes care of us. However, sweating to earn our daily bread shows appreciation to God for what He has done for us. Aiming to utilise the health and strength that God has given us to obtain our daily bread is actually a blessing for us.

As Christians, we need to prepare ourselves fully at every moment to do things to enable us to fulfil our destiny. This cannot be achieved by anything else other than equipping ourselves with the Word of God, so that when God is ready, He can move us according to His Word. Unfortunately, since we do not know our goals and do not know that God has called us for a purpose, we do not budget our time for anything and set the right goals, so we fail in life. We should be as good as Christ. We cannot achieve this unless we examine the past things that we used to do, for this will help us assess our present situation since we came to Christ.

These past things are the bad things such as our bad characteristics before we came to Christ. These never help us grow, since they will not let us make use of our talents to make our life successful. These talents are the natural gifts, strength and ability that God has given to us to live. However, when we are not able to make use of these gifts because of our bad characteristics, then we will fail in life. As followers of Christ, there will be nothing new and no change in our life since we came to Christ, and we will always be the same in the present as in our past. Our bad characteristics constantly stunt our growth, making us ineffective and inefficient.

Many characteristics influence our growth

Laziness is one of the major Christian mission hindrances because it contributes to the failure of our progress. As Christians, we should be hardworking, honest and keen to grow. It is our duty to progress in life, both spiritually and physically. We will be able to offer patience and commitment, to stand up to any challenging forces, and gain our achievement and progress. Many of us, however, do not want to work, not knowing that God gives us life and energy every day to work and earn our daily bread, so that we will give Him the glory. We should know the joy of our salvation; however, unfortunately, we have let worldly pleasures take it from us, because of our laziness. So, we do not enjoy the full salvation given to us by God. This laziness causes us so many problems that influence us in many ways. It even stops us from praying and sharing with other people of God.

Praying is the act of speaking or offering worship to God. Praying to God with faith will help us overcome every difficult situation and allow us to fulfil our mission with the help of the Holy Spirit. Prayer is one of the master keys to our Christian growth, but can be effective only if we do the will of God. Nowadays, we might pray a great deal, rather than do the work of God, but nothing good happens. There is no manifestation of the Word of God. We use most of our time praying, thinking that this is more important than doing God's work; we concentrate on praying instead of acting on and putting into practice the Word of God. It is doing the work of God that makes prayer manifest and effective.

Prayer opens doors to anything. However, failure to do God's work will have an ineffective result. This is why, now, we do not experience or get what we request in our prayers, despite our continued fasting and praying.

We should note that the spiritual aspect of matters is God's responsibility. Our responsibility is to put God's Word into practice. It is in putting into practice God's Word that we are equipped to fulfil our mission. Therefore, we must forget spiritual things and focus on practical things. Having done that, spiritual things become a bonus for us, through the work of the Holy Spirit. Practical and spiritual matters are important in our Christian life. However, practical matters are more important than spiritual or theoretical matters. The practical application of what we know about the Word of God will help us solve problems. It will definitely enable us to perform marvellous works, since God is more interested in our practical application of His Word, to bear witness to save people's lives. It is unfortunate that we lack this kind of prayer.

This lack of prayer may be caused by so many things that have a huge effect on our Christian development. At times, it is not we who do not wish to pray, but a situation that compels us to avoid praying. Sometimes daily pressures take our attention more than prayer. Some of us do not know how effective prayer can be, since there is not enough teaching about this. We are not taught that the Word of God will let us know the main ingredients of prayer or about the benefits of effective prayer. We focus on the prayer rather than its ingredients. Prayer works as long as we act on it. Many of us think that praying regularly, without stopping doing the things we did in the darkness of the past, will be effective. Some of us also think that praying is more important that putting God's Word into practice.

Sharing is a big problem, even within the ministry of Christ. We fail to progress because of a lack of sharing. Sharing is necessary in Christianity, because it is the root of love and it enables people to relate to each other. It brings joy, encouragement, appreciation, and forgiveness which brings reconciliation and brings people back into former relationships.

One of our downfalls is *hypocrisy or partiality*. We pretend to be very good or pretend to be what we are not, when we are not good and may have done something bad. This hypocrisy also causes a downfall in our development.

Sometimes, we do not keep an open mind about matters before making decisions, in order to get the right result which will help our growth. Many of us take sides in matters, before making judgements. However, for any right outcome, an open and impartial mind is needed. It means not showing more favour to any person or side than to others. This open-mindedness will lead to the right result in any situation. Therefore, if we want to develop both spiritually and physically, then we have to clarify the truth of a situation. Impartiality will make issues quite clear, and enable us to grow into true and mature Christians, because it allows the truth of the Word of God to be manifest to us. In order to see the function of God's Word and to maintain the credibility of the Gospel, our religious teachings and our attitudes must have this basis of truth.

Envy also hugely damages our Christian development. Some people always try to destroy others or wish their downfall, since they want other people's success or progress for themselves. It is not only people outside but even inside the body of Christ. Some of us are full of envy when we find out how our friends or other people are progressing; we try to destroy them in any manner, because we envy them. We try to be nice to others, but inwardly we are envious. This envy is a sin that prevents our Christian growth, since it indicates that we are still the same as before we came to Christ. In fact, envy can also be described as hatred. Any of us who hate others are enemies. The Bible always tells us to love our enemies. Sadly, that is not the case when it is Christians who do not like others. So, as Christians, where do we stand? We need to be different from our past; we have to refrain from the things we did in our past. However, envy has become a characteristic of Christians, and prevents us from experiencing the presence and power of God. If we do not change, then the Spirit of God cannot fall on us, make us new and fill us with

God. We will be unable to experience the presence and power of God, and unable to glorify God's name.

Lack of forgiveness means not getting rid of others' mistakes or sins against us. Our lack of forgiveness prevents us from working towards the life of God. It is a bad characteristic that is adverse to our growth. It causes a separation between God and us, and breaks the relationship between the people of God. It disturbs our worship of God and acts as an obstacle to our Christian mission. Since it has this effect, God asks us to free ourselves from this. However, some of our brothers' and sisters' mistakes or sins are difficult to forgive or forget. At the same time, the Lord asks us to do away with any sins against us, and not even have hard feelings towards these people. The Almighty God who created us asks us to forgive anyone who sins against us, because He always forgives our sins. He also says that it is a sin not to forgive. Therefore, if we refuse to forgive those who sin against us, then we do not really love the Lord but rather hate Him. We cannot love God whom we cannot see, and hate our brothers and sisters around us. If we adopt this unforgiving habit, then we are liars, whatever we may do in God's ministry. This lack of forgiveness of people's mistakes and sins causes us many problems that influence our growth. It also drives us to fulfil our own purpose instead of God's purpose. Then we will always have hardships, which do us no good in the long run.

Family is considered to be the basic root of life, and actually has an impact on human life. Without family, our lives would be miserable, because family has a great influence on most human activities.

A typical example of this is the marriage of our children. Often we do not wish our children to get married, thinking that a particular family are devils. However, this should not be the case. With family love, we are always looking at our children's future. If we are not convinced that their future will be all right, then we step in to thwart that thing from happening. In fact, most of these cases are based on love that the parents have for their children.

However, children are not aware of their parents' love for them. Even if they are, they want to do whatever they wish, and this may cause problems. At times, their family oppose the things that they want to do. Family causes many of the problems that we face. The problems may occur because of family ambition. It may happen that the family does not agree with the things that we want to do and achieve in life. Some families do not recognise the importance of self-decision, and do not allow their children to make their own decisions, thinking that they have more experience than their child. Therefore, their children are obliged to listen to them.

Many families do not know the importance of the Gospel, because of the malpractice of some Christians, and as a result, are determined not to allow their children to be involved in God's ministry. These malpractices have put families off encouraging our children to become Christians.

It is very disappointing to see that some families think Christians serve God with the body rather than with the heart, thinking that the Gospel has become a fashion. Some people use it to deceive others, in order to achieve their own personal interest. Some of the problems that we face from our families are because of religious differences. Some parents consider it very important to be in the same religion as their children, so, when this is not the situation, problems come between them and their children. Others also think that their children are rushing in life, because of the wrong teaching of the Gospel and the bad influence of other Christians; this causes hardship for our children in the long run. Some families are not interested in their children becoming Christians, and so many problems arise, which may influence us both spiritually and physically.

Lack of finance means that our levels of money are so low that we cannot even help ourselves in order to help others. The Word of God has nothing to do with money. However, in this world now, everything depends on money and nothing else. Hence, this lack of finance causes us huge problems, which are a hindrance to our mission. The number of Christians affected by low finances is rising all the time and many people are at risk.

In the house of God, the rise in the number of Christians living in poverty is partly because of other Christians. They do not let others understand that our success depends not on God, but on our own efforts. So we need to concentrate our efforts in order to cater for ourselves and others. We take responsibility for our own lives and act urgently and work seriously to improve our lives and help others. Doing that will greatly help, because it will influence people's lives, by turning their minds from the things that will not do them good. Most of us think that doing work is a worldly thing, so we do not want to work hard or work at all. Work will make us healthier and safer in life; it will not let us down, but help us fulfil our ambitions.

In addition, we do not make use of the little money we have by investing it, or putting money somewhere in order to obtain a profit in future. There are many way of investing; some of these are buying bonds, and establishing a company. These two methods will produce a profit in the short- or long-term. Once the money is invested, it will yield a better income or profit than the other. For instance, using money to set up a company can help people get jobs, so that they can earn their daily bread and even help others. At the same time, the company can produce profits that can also be used to help people who are at risk from disease and famine.

Churches always ask to contribute to the church, so that it can move on. Yet they do not want to use the money that they have accumulated to create jobs, even for those Christians who are poor. They think that jobs are worldly, but they welcome the money from those who are doing these jobs. They may forget that the money comes from the world and the jobs that the Christians are doing. On the other hand, what is the purpose of keeping money in the bank or for buying shares, without even using the profit to save people's lives? Furthermore, this even contributes to the poverty of the Christians who always bring the little they earn from their jobs, hoping that it will be used to save people's lives. Unfortunately, that is not the case: the money just accumulates in the bank for something else. We should be the largest donors of cash, food and materials, to assist people who are at risk of dying from poverty, disease and famine. Truly, we have a moral responsibility to help people and save their lives; it is our task, and it is what Christianity is all about. All these problems of low Christian finances do influence our growth and mission.

Another problem is *temptation*. There will be trials and temptations for us at every moment. There are many challenges in being Christians. We are supposed to stand up to challenges in our life. However, it can never be possible to overcome these challenges without fearing, obeying and trusting God. With the tremendous ability given to us by the Lord, we can do extremely well in Christ's ministry, and by doing such things, we will be able to thank God.

Fearing God

This means deeply respecting God and living by the Word of God. The fear of God does not necessarily mean that we are afraid of God as of other people; however, it implies that we acknowledge God and are determined to worship Him. It is an attitude of respect, responding to the Creator of all things, God. It is an acknowledgement of good intentions before God (Exodus 20:20) and makes a person receptive: *The fear of the Lord is the beginning of knowledge. (Proverbs 1:7)*. The fear of God also involves the fear of the consequences of disobedience. At times, temptation may occur when we may forget some of the vital reasons for obeying God, and do not think about its consequences. It is very good to fear God, because we can rid ourselves of the sinful natural body and soul that we inherit from the punishment of Adam and Eve, when they sinned against God; it can help us to work and live in holiness to achieve our salvation: *perfecting holiness in the fear of God. (2 Corinthians 7:1.* The purpose of the fear of God is that we trust and believe in God, and are willing and committed to live in God's way by doing what He says and obeying all His laws and commandments. We will have a peaceful mind, and live in love and joy in everlasting life.

Obeying God

This means respecting God and doing His will, acting in obedience to the rules and orders of God. Surely, the Lord desires docility from His people, as all parents desire obedience from their children. Our obedience to God and His work is the response to the calling of being a genuine Christian. The Word of God says that "to obey is better than sacrifice". We cannot be Christians without doing God's will.

The Bible states that there are true Christians and false Christians. True Christians have an attitude of respect and a response to God the Creator and Redeemer: *Blessed is everyone who fears the Lord, who walks in His ways. (Psalm 128:1).* We need to put our own will aside and put on the will of God. False Christians do not want to change, and are still the same as when they came to Christ. They do not obey God or do His work, thinking that their position in the church or contribution to the church, such as money and work, make them true Christians.

Trusting God

This means having confidence in God and His Word. It is feeling confident always that God exists and that His word is true, even though we have not seen Him physically. Trust is similar to hope. It means having strength to keep on going, having confidence and not letting our hearts be troubled in hard times, knowing that the Lord will not let us down. It is hoping that something good will come out of bad situations. Trust is being proud of ourselves, and enjoying life all the time, since we understand that we are blessed through the blood of the Lord Jesus Christ. Also, it can mean depending on God in accordance with His doctrine, rather than depending on ourselves or human expectations. We should know that the Lord we worship is a reliable God and responsible for His word, and that He is God who will never forsake us, neither will He leave us, especially in times of trouble:

Be strong and of good courage, do not fear nor be afraid of them: for the Lord your God, He is the one who goes with you. He will not leave you nor forsake you. (Deuteronomy 31:6)

So, if we are looking to make a real difference to our growth, we should focus on fearing, obeying and trusting God. Applying these words in our life will allow us to find out more about God and His Gospel. It will also lead us to find ourselves under the guidance and support of God, through the manifestation of the Holy Spirit.

Others, such as elders, leaders and friends, can also cause obstacles to our Christian mission. In fact, some elders and friends are not encouraging at all, because of their character, attitude or aim in the body of Christ. Our character and attitude are very important, since they determine what we are. They distinguish us totally from each other, and help us know the true Christians. In addition, our character and attitude influence the people of God around us, in deciding whether they should come to Christ or not. Any negative character or attitude discourages the growth of people around us and puts them in a difficult situation.

It is very surprising that some elders and leaders in the body of Christ fight for membership and for position. This intense fighting creates a humanitarian disaster for other people of God and causes a hugely detrimental effect to the Gospel. These battles occur because of the desire for achievement of our personal purposes. This problem forces many of us to flee Christ's ministry to the world in which we lived before we came to Christ. Others also claim to be the owners of the churches of Christ, instead of the Lord being the owner. Truly, it is publicly known that any church where the Gospel of Jesus Christ is preached belongs to God. Therefore, the Lord Jesus Christ is the owner of that church and the church belongs to the public. This is not the case sometimes, even though the Lord's Name is always pronounced as if the Lord is the head and owner of the church. Inwardly, the church is someone's property and controlled by a few people. We, the other members of the church, are not allowed to express our views or concerns. Christians who claim to be the owners of the church usually want people to listen to them. Whatever they say is final, whether it is good or bad; nobody has the chance to freely express their views on church matters.

These kinds of people can be seen as extremists, doing things contrary to Christ's religion, but claiming to be the true born-again Christians, filled with the Holy Spirit. Their preaching or teaching is indirectly different from Christ's teachings or religion. They are the types of people who do not want to tell the truth or admit that something has gone wrong. It is good to see Christians admitting that a problem in God's ministry needs to be solved or tackled, in order to promote the Gospel's growing reputation to save lives.

If we examine their characters carefully, we can see that they aim to use the Lord's Name for their own personal purpose. What they are doing in Christ's ministry is causing the downfall of others. What we should do is ask ourselves what we really need to do that will enable our growth, and see what others around us can do. These problems continue to cause hardship for God's people and worry in God's ministry. We are largely to blame for the lack of Gospel development. All these problems in Christ's ministry block our Christian growth as well as our gift of ministry, which is our spiritual structure in life. The cause of all these crises is the personal purposes of some Christians, rather than God's purposes. This brings shame on the entire ministry. So, for us to progress and fulfil our Gospel purpose, it is strongly recommended that the committed leaders should come down very heavily on those people who engage in any malpractice, and make sure that they are suitably punished.

In addition, if we want to maintain Gospel credibility and improve our standards, we should continue to work to provide efficient, professional and sensitive service for the entire Christian body. This is because the main root of the problems is the misunderstanding of the Bible and Christ's teachings. We are always undermined by the failure to teach and preach the true Gospel. Those who teach the Bible and preach the message should always come clean about it, and work exactly from the Bible, so that they do not mislead others. We should continue our desire for the worship of God, and ensure that our dedication, commitment and motivation are always for the Gospel. We must be honest and ensure that our aims, hopes and desires are to save people's lives.

The churches of God have to be vital sources of support and encouragement for Christians, and for non-Christians who are unable to cope independently, in their spiritual and physical as well as social needs. We have to do this, to demonstrate our moral responsibility and commitment to help the people of God, for their lives to be saved. Doing this will help us overcome our mission hindrance, so that we can grow and do our Gospel work effectively and efficiently to save people's lives.

God's Followers

And as He walked by the Sea of Galilee, He saw Simon and Andrew his brother casting a net into the sea; for they were fishermen. Then Jesus said to them, "Follow Me, and I will make you become fishers of men." They immediately left their nets and followed Him. (Mark 1: 16–18)

Then Jesus said to those Jews who believed Him, "If you abide in my Word, you are My disciples indeed. And you shall know the truth, and the truth shall make you free." (John 8: 31–2)

We have a real relationship with God and experiences of seeing the glory of God in our life. Followers accept doing someone else's wish, they are devoted to a particular person and they believe in their actions. That person assists them and provides moral support, regardless of circumstances. They are totally committed to the one they follow and believe in the outcome of what they do.

Who are God's followers? God's followers do the will of God. We do the same things as Christ, and understand that we are obliged to do the will of God, without having a choice. The typical examples of followers are the disciples of Christ. To follow someone is very important, because it does not mean taking for granted what they do. Before following someone, we need to know the reason why we follow them, its importance and its effects. It is a matter of trust and commitment: if we trust somebody, we will commit to and rely on them. We followers of Christ have moved away from our past life and put on the life of Christ, our present life. The Word of God prevails in our mind, and we make a positive impact on people's lives by showing the love of Jesus Christ. We understand the Gospel and are always willing to carry out our Gospel task.

We are devoted to God and totally believe in His teachings. If we are devoted, we have decided to act in accordance with the Word of God, and have taken God as our everything. We have closed out everything else, and given ourselves up to a particular purpose. The main difference is that we have changed our life. We have an emphasis on repentance and willingness to do God's work. We have finally decided to follow Christ, by believing in Him and abiding in His Word. These two elements show that we are fully committed to God immediately after baptism by water. We totally empty ourselves for the Gospel. We can also be called disciples.

We disciples have turned from the sins we have committed, we keep all God's statutes and do what is lawful and right. The Bible states that we shall surely live, and we shall not die for ever, since we do these things. We love God and keep His Word. We are true and honest Christians, and our lives demonstrate the life of Christ. This is seen through our thoughts, words and deeds. We really understand the Gospel and its aims. We value the Word of God and do not preach the Gospel in just any old manner: we talk about God. We are termed born-again Christians. We are committed and determined to obey what the Bible says. The disciples were committed and determined to follow Jesus, no matter what would happen, even though, at times, they experienced hardship that discredited them. As far as people are concerned, they were outstanding followers of Christ.

We understand that God is our light and salvation, and the strength of our life. We constantly have confidence in the Lord, even when we encounter many problems. We know that God is our helper and salvation; therefore, God will never leave or forsake us. God will take care of us, even if our parents forsake us because we apply the Word of God to our life and have an unusual faith in God. We make a positive decision to dwell in the house of God all the days of our life. We are always keen to improve our physical and spiritual lives, because, without taking this into consideration, we cannot fulfil our Gospel mission on this earth. We believe that 'what goes around, comes around': whatever we do on this earth, we will account for before we die. We seek to have God teach and lead us on a smooth path, so that we do not perish. We will not do the will of our adversaries and lose God's Grace.

There are many characteristics of good followers; Psalm 15 reveals people who are determined to learn from God:

He who walks uprightly, and works righteously, and speaks the truth in his heart; He who does not backbite with his tongue, nor does evil to his neighbour, nor does he take up a reproach against his friend; In whose eyes a vile person is despised, but he honours those who fear the Lord … He who does these things shall never be moved. (Psalms 15: 2–5)

We are totally aware that, because of our character, we will not be removed from the house of the Lord. We are upright and righteous; we are truthful and do not bite back with our tongues. We do no evil to anyone, nor do we take up a reproach against our neighbour. We always honour people who fear God, and if we are hurt by others, we do not retaliate. We do not put out our money with usurers, and do not bribe innocent people.

Backsliders

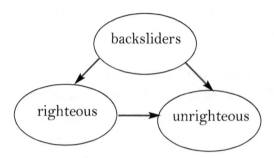

2.7: Backsliders

Backsliding is going back into wrongdoing. Who are backsliders? They are people who believe in God and used to go to church; however, they have stopped attending church for some reason. Backsliders do wrong things or have gone back to their past wrongdoings, their past life or old bad habits. Even regular churchgoers or Christians can become backsliders. The term may also apply to people who always attend church but do not follow the Word of God. Any people who backslide are in a very dangerous situation, because they may go back and do more bad things than before.

There are two types, *righteous* and *unrighteous*, as the above diagram shows. *Righteous* do the right thing about their backsliding. They believe in God and understand the principles of the Word of God; this implies that they fear God and always do their best to obey the Ten Commandments. With *righteous backsliders*, the Holy Spirit is in control. Since the Holy Spirit is truly present in their life, such backsliders are likely to experience the presence of the Holy Spirit in their life, moving them in the right direction. This is very effective and the outcome is good, despite some difficulties that may occur. Though they do not attend church any more, they enjoy the benefits of the Gospel, they can always say that God exists and they have confidence in Him. Such backsliders are far better than the backsliding churchgoers. Because the Holy Spirit is experienced by righteous backsliders, they are more able to stand against any problems they may encounter than unrighteous backsliders, as they are stable in difficult situations, believing that God is in control.

Unrighteous backsliders can be called sinful people, since they have gone back to their old life and do even worse things than in the past. They believe in God but cannot get rid of their past life. They may understand the principles of the Word of God; however, one way or another, they are very interested in the things of the world. They do not fear God and do things that are contrary to the Ten Commandments. With unrighteous backsliders, the Holy Spirit is present but He has no control of the backsliders' life, compared with that of righteous backsliders. It is the things that the unrighteous backsliders do, which are contrary to the Gospel, that block the functioning of the Holy Spirit. This situation is hardly going to bear good fruit.

Backsliding does not just happen, but has a cause; finding the cause is the key to solving the problem. One cause might be problems that they may have encountered in their life, especially in the body of Christ. Another cause may be laziness.

What can be done about it? Firstly, the church or church authority can forbid them from attending. This does not happen regularly, because most believers, especially the church authorities, always do their best to cope with difficult situations.

Secondly, the backsliders may dislike worshipping God with other Christians or attending church, since they find unpleasant things about them. One outstanding thing about backsliders is that, as time goes on, they can go back to worshipping God, not necessarily at the same church as before, but somewhere else.

Backsliding Churchgoers and Non-Churchgoers

Backsliding churchgoers can also be called backsliding Christians. They usually go to church but have not refrained from their past life. They do whatever they like, regardless of Gospel principles. At times, they believe that so long as they have been baptised, that is the end of their Christian journey, and they are automatically classified as disciples since they are already in Heaven. They do not understand that becoming Christians is an acceptance of the invitation to become disciples of Christ. An invitee has to fulfil something: doing the will of God rather than doing their own will, which is just like being in the world, with nothing to do with the Word of God.

Many things can cause Christians to become backsliding churchgoers; however, their spiritual growth is the main one. If Christian spirits or souls are immature, then they have not grown enough for the Holy Spirit to take control of those particular Christians. Then it is likely that they will be blown and tossed about by any wave of the world that can lead them to backslide, since the Word of God cannot work effectively, or even work at all. Because of the failure of the Holy Spirit to take control of those particular Christians' lives to overcome the crisis they may encounter, they will have no alternative but to backslide. Other things can cause us to backslide, since our spiritual growth depends on them: not educating ourselves through the Word of God, not having a strong belief in our actions, not exercising God's Word in our own life, lack of prayer, lack of determination, and lack of patience.

Spiritual growth is one of the most important factors for us to survive our Christian journey. It allows us to stand against any problems of this world and focus only on the Word of God. The Holy Spirit normally works in His own way, but can work better if our spirit is mature. Spiritual growth is to do with faith and assurance; therefore, if our spirit has grown, nothing can cause us to backslide. We may be affected one way or another, since the Holy Spirit provides an effective influence on us, enabling us to focus on God only and stand firm, no matter what happens to us. Spiritually grown Christians are those of us who understand what Christianity is about and what we have involved ourselves in.

Backsliding non-churchgoers believe in God and used to go to church. However, they have stopped attending church for some reason. The backsliding non-churchgoers contain two types, namely righteous backsliders and unrighteous backsliders.

Unbelievers

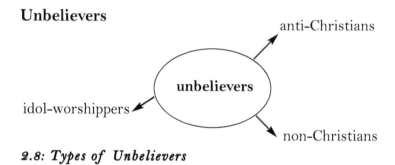

anti-Christians

unbelievers

idol-worshippers

non-Christians

2.8: Types of Unbelievers

For many deceivers have gone out into the world who do not confess Jesus Christ as coming in the flesh. This is a deceiver and an antichrist. (2 John 1:7)

Anti-Christians are those who either oppose Christ or deny Him, and are great enemies of Christ and His Gospel. They are people who do not believe in Jesus Christ and His Gospel, who have no faith in Christ, and who refuse to believe in Him and His religion. They feel no duty and responsibility to believe in God and His Word, or to study, learn and put it into practice. They may hear the Gospel of Christ, read the Bible and Christian books, do charity work, and love and care for other people. However, they are not believers, because they do not believe in God and refuse to accept Jesus Christ as their personal Saviour. The acceptance of Christ as personal Saviour is not the only condition of being believers: the most important condition is the acceptance and belief in God as the creator of everything and the father of Jesus Christ. Unbelievers do the will of Satan rather than the will of God, and they feel free to do whatever they like.

They stand against Christians, and their mission is to destroy the work of God, in order to promote the work of Satan. They constantly find ways to deceive Christians, to enable Satan to destroy those Christians or become his followers. Therefore, they are constantly determined to work hard, to confuse the people of God, by creating problems in our daily lives. Their aim is to make us join the kingdom of Hell that is inherited by Satan. They stand totally against the Word of God, and therefore do not like us Christians, and they all seem to have the same mission. We Christians do the work of God; therefore, if they oppose us, then they oppose God. They work for Satan, so they always aim to destroy our Christian ambitions.

However, they might study God's Word, read the Bible and Christian books, to equip themselves to do their work. They come into the Kingdom of God and mix with us true Christians, but have a different agenda, since their aim is contrary to that of true Christians. It is hard to identify anti-Christians; it takes the work of the Holy Spirit alone, since they come in to the Kingdom of God with a strategy for their work.

They are on the mission of Satan, and must fulfil and accomplish it. This activity can take place especially in the church of Christ, so the Bible shows us. The responsibility for dealing with anti-Christians lies with us true Christians, because anti-Christians have the characteristics of true Christians. So we have the right and power to deal with anti-Christians if we notice their behaviour, before they destroy other Christians' lives. We all experience some woes of the world, such as sickness, poverty and distress. Since unbelievers do not believe in and rely on the Word of God, it is likely that they cannot stand up to all these woes. As a result of not knowing that God keeps us safe, they are unhappy, give up easily and at times they take their own lives.

Non-Christians may be at variance with Christian principles; however, they believe in God. They have faith in God but have not accepted Jesus Christ as their personal Saviour. Non-Christians might one way or another becomes Christian believers. However, it would be very difficult for anti-Christians to become Christians, because they totally hate Christians and God, and have a different agenda to fulfil.

Idol worshippers worship other gods, though they may also believe in God or Christ. They worship idols because they believe that the idols can cater for their daily needs; they do this also for protection and breakthrough.

3 Gospel Benefits

And of His fullness we have all received, and grace for grace. For the law was given through Moses, but grace and truth came through Jesus Christ. (John 1:16–17)

God ◄———(Gospel benefits)———► humans

3.1: Gospel Benefits to God and Humans

Benefit means something that is good for humankind and that promotes people's wellbeing. The Gospel is God's Word. There are so many benefits; some of them are power, peace and help.

There are two categories of gospel benefits above: those that are to do with God and those that benefit humans. The former ones show the nature of God. They can truly help us, God's people, to take the Gospel seriously. We can make any breakthrough in our lives, by concentrating on these three Gospel benefits to God. There is a purpose for everything we do and see around us, and there are reasons for the Gospel and the coming of Christ. God sent Jesus Christ to this earth for a reason. It is this reason that we should think about and focus on, more than anything else in this world. If we concentrate on them, they will provide us with all the Gospel benefits that we need.

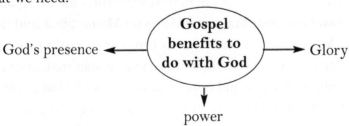

God's presence ◄———(Gospel benefits to do with God)———► Glory

power

3.2: Gospel Benefits to do with God

93

God's presence

This is to do with holy fear, and demonstrates that God is present everywhere. Therefore, we must fear Him, obey Him and follow His Ten Commandments. The presence of God reminds all of us children of God not to do sinful things and to be as holy as God Himself.

Glory

God always shines around His people. The glory of God shows God's appearance to us on every occasion. This glory can be seen both physically and spiritually; at times, it shines like a sun or a light. It can come in any form, by fire or light. The most important thing is that the Gospel is the key way for God to show us His glory. Without this, it may be hard for God to show His glory to us, or for us to understand it.

Power

God has more power than anyone; nothing compares with God. This power explains what God is like. It moves everywhere to heal and cleanse people. These things are done to show God's grace, and to assure us that nothing is too difficult for God to do, or for us to do. We are created through Him, who created everything and who does all things.

Then there are the benefits for humans from the Gospel of Christ. These result from the blood of Jesus Christ, and cover the entire doctrine of God. This doctrine refers to the ten rules for living and for worship that God made known to Moses on Mount Sinai, and the teachings of Jesus Christ. These benefits bring great profit to all of us. However, before we can benefit, we have to be committed, to work hard, have faith, confidence and hope, and be doers of God's work. We need to be determined to give our life to God completely, so that He will control our body and soul. We cannot practise the work of

God, without comparing our past and present life. Some of us think that as soon as we become Christians, we do not have to think about our past. This thought has become a philosophy in the body of Christians, and it influences Christian growth. Yet for us Christians, the difference between our past and present life is very important, because it lets us know whether or not we have changed the bad things we did, since we came to God. In addition, comparing past and present enables us to examine ourselves, in order to get rid of things that are contrary to the Word of God. Thus we are able to do God's work and become genuine Christians. Some Christians say that the Bible tells us not to think about our past. This is true in term of self-condemnation: if we condemn ourselves for past things, then we will not be able to concentrate and worship God, and are no longer useful. This arrests our Christian development and prevents us from obtaining Gospel benefits.

Removal of Burdens, Salvation and Eternal Life

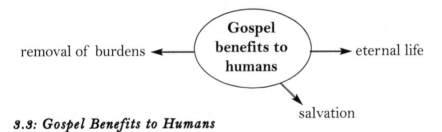

3.3: Gospel Benefits to Humans

Removal of burdens

If we become Christians, a burden is taken off us. This could be a burden of sorrow, of debts or of sin, anything that can ruin us. Before we come to Christ, we carry a burden every moment of our life. This retards our progress, since it does not allow us to achieve a successful life, It is the responsibility of the Lord to deal with it. He can tackle this problem only if we become Christians, and are willing to do His work.

Salvation

Salvation is the renewal and restoration of humankind from our loss through the fall of Adam and Eve. It is the spiritual blessings on us that come from Jesus Christ and our deliverance from the effects of sin.

Eternal life

This is to do with our present life and future life. Our present life is the new Christian life that we have received in Jesus Christ. This brings peace, joy, love and authority in this world. Our future life is the life to come, the reward by God for all Christians. It is our inheritance from almighty God, which is heaven. Heaven is the new Kingdom promised to human kind, based on the assessment of all of us Christians on this earth. Our qualification to achieve eternal life depends on our ability and hard work. To be in the new Kingdom, we have to be true Christians, determined to let our life be like Christ's life. We look forward to the coming of Christ, and have the confidence that enables us to stand firm and fight for our success, to finish the Gospel race. We are always determined and willing to keep up the good work, as is required of us by the Bible. We also believe that, whatever happens, whether we like it or not, the world will come to an end, therefore doing the work of God is our main priority.

Gospel Tokens

Gospel tokens are defined as the Gospel bonus, and the fruits of the Gospel. These refer to spiritual things, yet they deal with physical matters as well. They are the bonus of the Gospel, because it is given freely to us, in addition to our life being saved. They are given by God through His Gospel, to prove His love, His power and protection. Their main goal is to promote the Gospel of Christ, to save the life of God's people, as well as helping us receive God's heritage.

However, this ambition cannot be successful if we live just in our flesh. This is a natural disease that we inherit through birth. There are two types of birth, one physical and the other spiritual. Physical birth is normal birth through our mothers and fathers; it happens through the will of a man and a woman. Anyone who is born of the will of a man and woman is born of flesh, unless God comes through, since the Bible states that unless we are born again, we can never enter the kingdom of God. On the other hand, the will of the flesh must be cured, before we can praise God and be entitled to the Gospel token. This curing of the flesh can only be achieved through the acceptance of God, as a result of our changing our will for God's will.

With spiritual birth, it is the acceptance of Jesus Christ as our personal Saviour through baptism. If we are born again, it simply means we are willing to do the work of God. In fact, it is not baptism that makes Christians, but doing the work of God.

Below are the Gospel tokens to which we are entitled for our Gospel race:

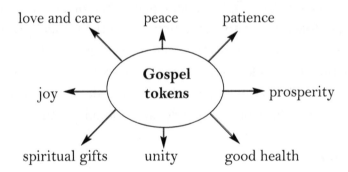

3.4: Gospel Tokens

Joy

This is gladness, and is one of the fruits of the Spirit and is part of the character of God. By becoming Christians and doing the work of God, we will feel confident in all our doings, and this makes us always happy. We are supposed to experience this kind of joy, no matter what our circumstances. We have to feel full of joy, as well as feel at peace all the time, whether or not everything in our life is going well.

Love and care

These are the roots of the Gospel, because it is through these that Jesus Christ came to save humankind. He physically emphasised this love and care for other people all the time, to let us know its importance to the Gospel and to humankind. Love is essential and valuable, so nothing can buy it. If we love somebody, we care for them as well. It is not surprising that we get this love from doing the work of God; since we do the work of God, this love is given to us by God, to let us as well as the public know the God we worship. Doing God's work lets us know our need to love our fellow humans and care for them.

Peace

This is freedom from fighting and quarrelling of any kind. Peace as a Gospel token refers to a situation where the Gospel prevents the stress of woes and gives us the assurance of success. These woes are trouble, distress, sickness and poverty, for example. The Bible shows that, through Jesus Christ, peace has been made with God. The Word of God lets us have one Lord, one faith and one birth.

Patience

This helps us greatly in life. It contributes to problem-solving and opens a channel to success in life. We have patience; we succeed in most cases, since we have control over things that annoy or trouble us, that can lead us into risky situations. It is very sad that sometimes we do not have this kind of patience, as our master Jesus Christ did. Through this patience, Jesus Christ, the Lord Himself bore our sins and died for us on the cross without complaining. It was love and patience that opened a way for the Lord to fulfil His mission for His children.

His devotion to us was the great example of human kindness and patience. We need patience in all our doings, in order to go further in achieving our aims, as the Lord demonstrated to us. We have to calmly endure every situation with this patience, without complaining or losing self-control, and believe in the Lord, because it is He who knows what is going to happen in our future. Only our Maker knows what is good for us at times, in what we think are terrible situations. Our desire is not His desire.

Prosperity

This means having success. The Bible makes it clear that whatever we do, we shall prosper. Prosperity does not mean money or financial blessings, but other factors that make us succeed in life. One of the factors that can bring prosperity is peace. This promise of prosperity is subject to one condition, that we do the good work of the Gospel. We have to put away bad things and put on good things. This will enable us to follow in the footsteps of Christ, making us more and more like Jesus Christ, the Lord. With this promise and by doing the work of God, there is no doubt that we will succeed in life and in our doings.

Good health

This maintains peace, which will provide good health, helping us live a long life, to fulfil the purpose that God has for His people.

Unity

This is one of the important parts of the Gospel of Christ, because it expresses our love for each other. It shows us that we have a single God, birth, church, and one faith. Also, it allows us to partake of one food and to have one hope. Truly, we need to express our views and experiences in the body of Christ, in order to bring unity to Christ's churches.

Many Christians believe that it is impossible for the churches of Christ to be united, because the Bible states this. We take the Gospel for granted by doing whatever we want. If we Christians cannot be united, what is the purpose of being Christians, or the point of the church of God? We need to make an assessment of our Christianity: think about the value of the Gospel and the purpose of the crucifixion of Jesus Christ, which totally emphasises love and care for the people of God. Do we agree that we in the churches should not bother with unity? No, because if that is the case, then the coming of Christ and His crucifixion are useless.

The problem of unity is caused by some of us who use the Gospel to achieve our own personal ambitions. Also, some of us do not seek the Holy Spirit to monitor some of our religious behaviour, and so we do things that are not in accordance with God's will. Surely, unity is what we should all seek and do something about before anything else, since it demonstrates our true nature as followers of Christ and His Gospel. If we do not strongly unite, then our Gospel work is in vain, because Jesus Christ did not recommend that. It is merely human thinking, from a lack of deep understanding of the teachings of Christ. Many Christians use the language of human wisdom to teach, preach and do many things, rather than depending on the Holy Spirit.

4 Demonstration of Spirit

Introduction

What is a *spirit* and, in particular, what is *demonstration of spirit*? Spirit means the spiritual or immaterial part of a human being that is known as our soul. It feels, thinks and lets the body do things; anything that the body does, whether good or bad, depends on this.

A question for us to ask is: what are the types and sources of spirit? Source means the place where something comes from. We need to know and understand the origin of things, since it contributes greatly to our human life. The sources of spirit are the places where the spirit comes from. There are two main basic sources of spirit: one called God and the other Satan. The Spirit of God is made up of two: the human spirit and the Holy Spirit.

This chapter deals with what we do to allow ourselves to be filled with the Holy Spirit. This indicates that we need to be filled with another spirit, although we have a spirit already, the natural spirit. Our human spirit consists of good spirit and bad spirit, concerning good and bad things respectively. This chapter demonstrates many kinds of spirit and their function and effects on us.

Demonstration of spirit is used to describe a number of spirits that we possess or can be influenced by in our life. It lets us examine and test the spirit before we believe it or decide our ways of living, since there are many spirits in this world, which are not good to believe or follow. There are forces that constantly influence us in our everyday lives, in order to confuse and destroy us. The most vital aspect is the functions and outcome of the Spirit of God and the evil spirit.

Types of Spirits

For what man knows the things of a man except the spirit of the man which is in him? Even so no one knows the things of God except the Spirit of God. Now we have received, not the spirit of the world, but the Spirit who is from God, that we might know the things that have been freely given to us by God. (1 Corinthians 2: 11–12)

This tells us that there are many kinds of spirits but that the Holy Spirit functions differently.

Go therefore and make disciples of all nations, baptising them in the name of the Father and of the Son and of the Holy Spirit. (Matthew 28:19)

And the Lord God formed man of the dust of the ground, and breathed into his nostrils the breath of life; and man became a living being. (Genesis 2:7) Here, the breath of life indicates the Spirit of God.

A Demon-possessed Man was Healed.

He said to him, "Come out of the man, unclean spirit!" Then He asked him, "What is your name?" And he answered, saying, "My name is Legion; for we are many." (Mark 5: 8–9)

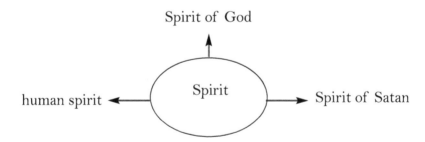

4.1: Demonstration of Spirit: God

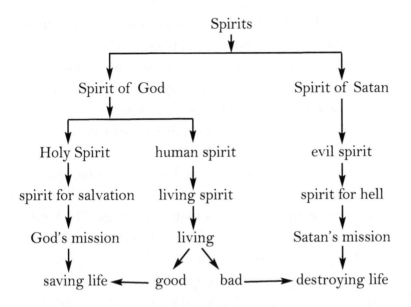

4.2: Demonstration of Spirits

Figures 4.1 and 4.2 above show two main types of spirits, their sources and characters, for us to understand in our daily life. They also help us to know the differences between them, enabling us to focus on the Gospel of Christ, if our ambition is to have a future life.

The two main types of spirit are the Spirit of God and the spirit of the world (evil spirit). The Spirit that comes from God can be considered to consist of two spirits, the human spirit and the Holy Spirit.

And all flesh died that moved on the earth: birds and cattle and beasts and every creeping thing that creeps on the earth, and every man. All in whose nostrils was the breath of the spirit of life, all that was on the dry land, died. (Genesis 7:21–22)

The human spirit is also known as the living spirit, natural spirit or spirit of life. This spirit enables us to breathe and be alive. In fact, our welfare on the earth totally depends on this spirit. It allows us to know the things that God has freely given to us.

This spirit is one; however, we have two choices. We may do good things or bad things. We all have two spirits, one good and the other bad. The good spirit lets the people of God to do good things, while the bad spirit lets us to do bad things. These two spirits normally attend on us all through our life. The good spirit that permits us to do good things is the Spirit of God, as shown in figure 4.1 above. The good spirit relates to the Holy Spirit. Any of us who do good things are entitled to receive blessings from the Lord, which, in most cases, are physical blessings or gifts of the Gospel, even though we may not be Christians.

The main function of the bad spirit is to do bad things. The Lord, our Father who created us, knows that if we do bad things, they will not help us, and might even lead us to death. This is Satan planning to destroy our life. Nobody can fight against Satan, conquer him and control this sin, except the Lord. The Lord knows that it is only He who can overcome and forgive this kind of sin inherited from Adam and Eve, and cleanse us of it forever. This issue of forgiveness and cleanness, termed salvation, is introduced by God in order to get rid of this sin. Therefore, God planned to save His children from this sin, by sending His son Jesus Christ to come and deliver us from sin through salvation. Salvation is the act of saving our soul, delivering us from sin and the punishment for sin, all by means of the Holy Spirit. This is through baptism, the moment we accept Jesus Christ as our personal saviour to do God's work.

We have two choices, whether to do good or bad things. We are not under any obligation to choose, for it is up to us to make a decision. In most cases we do both good and bad things. However, what we need to bear in mind is that whatever we do, we will be rewarded for it.

The spirit is given to all of us by God through birth, so we all have this spirit. God gives it, and if God takes this natural spirit from us, we will die. At death, the natural spirit leaves the body and returns to God. A ghost is the spirit of a dead person that has separated from the body. There are other names for the human spirits: natural spirit, human nature spirit and the living spirit.

The Holy Spirit is given to all of us, to help us complete our Gospel race. It deals with the Gospel of Christ and is a God-given Spirit. This Spirit is obtained from God when we accept Jesus Christ as our personal Saviour through baptism. It is the spirit given to us through Jesus to walk in (*Galatians 5: 16-26*).

There are numerous names for the Holy Spirit:
2 Timothy 1:7 - Spirit of love
Ephesians 4:30 - Spirit of God
John 14:17 - Spirit of truth
Romans 8:9 - Spirit of Christ
Isaiah 11:2 - Spirit of wisdom and understanding
Nehemiah 9:20 - good Spirit
Romans 8:2 - Spirit of life
Ephesians 1:13 - Spirit of promise
John 14:16 - the Comforter
Isaiah 11:2 –Spirit of counsel
Hebrews 10:9 - Spirit of grace.

The Holy Spirit enables us to know the things of God that have been freely given to us. It shows us specially the deep things of God. Both the Spirit of God (Holy Spirit) and human spirit come from God; however, it is only the Spirit of God that knows the things of God. Anyone who has this Spirit can experience the wisdom of God, which is the hidden wisdom or spiritual wisdom.

The Holy Spirit deals with holy things and it lets us feel and think about good things, making us act straightaway. It is the spirit of knowledge, wisdom, understanding, love, guidance, protection and love.

It is the Lord who gives this to us, and it is given under a contract, for us to do God's work, which is the Gospel. It is given at the moment that we accept Jesus Christ through baptism. We enter into a personal relationship with God, and are under a contract to perform our duty. If we fail to perform our duty, the Lord can take the Holy

Spirit from us.

On the other hand, when we refuse to put on good things, the manifestation of the Holy Spirit is not likely to be experienced. In this case, although God takes the Holy Spirit from us through our disobedience, we will still have life; we do not die physically. In fact, we all have this Holy Spirit; however, we cannot experience its manifestation if we continue not to do God's work.

It does not, however, mean that all human beings possess an evil spirit, which is witchcraft. Since Satan is always working against God's plan, doing bad things is considered to be the work of evil. Our human spirit is the spirit of choice, which is totally different from someone who possesses an evil spirit, which is commonly called witchcraft. Doing bad things, which is sin and the work of bad spirit, came to us as a punishment when Adam and Eve, our parents, sinned against God. The Bible states that our generation is full of sin; therefore, all of us on this earth have this kind of bad spirit that at times fights against God and His work.

An evil spirit is a spirit that we might inherit through family, friends or a relationship. It is also called a bad spirit and it is Satan who gives it. Its main aim is to destroy our lives. However, some people use it to charm in magic. It can be possessed by human beings, and can kill people, or influence them to destroy others. This type of possession is commonly known as witchcraft. This evil spirit can be possessed by both Christians and non-Christians. As the name indicates, people who possess it are likely to do bad things.

This evil spirit is like the human spirit, since it lets us feel, think and act. Whatever we may do, good or bad, in the end there will be destruction. Why is it so? The main aim of this spirit is to kill and destroy. Any people who possess an evil spirit do not practise righteousness; at times, they may do good things, but in the end, everything is in vain or results in destruction. It always puts them in a miserable situation, since its main work is to destroy humankind. This kind of spirit is very powerful, like the Holy Spirit. People who have this evil spirit can do similar things to the Holy Spirit. Only the

Lord through the Holy Spirit can get rid of the evil spirit, but only if those who possess the evil spirit are willing for this to happen.

It is very difficult to distinguish the works of this evil spirit from the works of the Holy Spirit. It takes only the Word of God to tackle this problem. The difference between the works of an evil spirit and of the Holy Spirit works can be determined only by us, who have moved away from our past and our bad doings. Only when we really do the work of God can we sense the difference between the Holy Spirit and an evil spirit.

The evil spirit lets us do bad things and leads us to nothing. It deals with the world and always aims to put us to shame and destruction. It creates fear, weakness and all sorts of negativity, in order to destroy us.

There are many names for the evil spirit:
1 John 4:3 - spirit of Anti-Christ
1 John 4:6 - spirit of error
Luke 8:2 - evil spirit
Mark 1:23 - unclean spirit
Revelation 16:14 - spirit of demons.

Fruits of the Spirits

Fruit is an outcome, and we need to know and understand the outcome of everything. The fruits of the spirits are the outcome of the various spirits, the human spirit, evil spirit and the Holy Spirit. There are many fruits of the evil spirit: to perform wonders, prophesy charm, bring a disruptive influence and bad advice, although the main fruits are to kill people, harm and charm them. This spirit at times influences people to ruin their happiness, and to equip them to stand against God, His work or His people.

The main fruit of the Holy Spirit is in providing God's spiritual gifts to us, to equip us for God's work. God gives these spiritual gifts to His children in many ways. Some of these gifts are preaching and teaching the Gospel, prophesying, healing, knowledge and wisdom.

Types of Spiritual Gifts

To one is given the word of wisdom through the Spirit, to another the word of knowledge through the same Spirit, to another faith by the same Spirit, to another the gift of healings by the same Spirit, to another the working of miracles, to another prophecy, to another discerning of spirits, to another different kinds of tongues, to another the interpretation of tongues. (1 Corinthians 12:8–10)

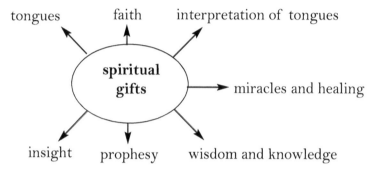

4.3: Types of Spiritual Gifts

Spiritual Gifts are given freely to us by God through the Holy Spirit. They are the fruit of the Holy Spirit and do similar work to the Holy Spirit; for example, they help us know the things of God.

It is one of the Gospel tokens that we are all entitled to them. They are some of the functions of the Word of God given to us, to save life, to proclaim the Gospel and to assist us in accomplishing our mission of the Gospel. They function differently; however, they all work to achieve the one ambition of the Gospel, to save people's lives. They enable us to experience the presence and power of God, and to continue our enjoyment of the Gospel. There are many ways that God gives them to us.

There are many types of spiritual gifts, as shown in figure 4.3 above. However, common spiritual gifts are as follows:

Tongues

The gift of tongues is defined as a message from God, a word sent from God to us, maybe about God's church. It is actually an inspired utterance by someone in an unknown language. If we speak in tongues, God speaks though us, and we have no idea what we will say, or what has been said. The words spoken need an interpreter to be present to explain the meaning to us. Whoever does this has to be appointed by God through the Holy Spirit. It is another way in which God speaks to us. It has nothing to do with wisdom and knowledge. Truly, any message from the Lord has a purpose, so speaking in tongues has a meaning and has to be interpreted. The interpreter tells us exactly what has been spoken; false interpretation may make the message useless and may also have a huge effect on the person who speaks in tongues. It would have a devastating effect on the people who are seeking God at that moment, because it would disregard God's manifestation of His power.

Prophecy

This gift is the foretelling of future events through speaking or writing. An example of a book of prophecy is the book of Isaiah. This gift can be seen as a gift of protection or progress, because it lets us know what is ahead, so that we can take precautions if it is a dangerous thing. This gift has nothing to do with prosperity and personality, nor does it classify the people prophesying as more important than others, for it has nothing to do with superiority or worldly matters.

It is not a common gift in the Kingdom of God, even though we are all entitled to receive it. Many of us rely on this gift, thinking that it will help us throughout our lives. Therefore, we wrongly depend on those who claim to have this kind of gift, instead of depending on God and His Word. Also, we aim to receive this gift, so that people around us may know that we are true Christians. However, it is very sad that we have no clue about how and where it can be received. In order to receive it, we have to do God's work. Doing God's work is not the same as doing church activities. It means understanding and carrying out Christian objectives, applying the Word of God to ourselves, experiencing it and carrying out the message to the public to save lives.

The gift has two aspects, bad and good. It is both dangerous and good, since it can kill and save life. If we have this gift, we must be very careful and wise indeed, because foretelling wrongly things that may cause someone's death or separation can have an effect on us too. Many people have this gift, but are not effective, because of their past lies, lying for fame, to condemn people, or to influence others.

Differences between the gifts of tongues and prophecy

Therefore tongues are for a sign, not to those who believe but to unbelievers; but prophesying is not for unbelievers but for those who believe. Therefore, if the whole church comes together in one place and all speak with tongues, and there come in those who are uninformed or unbelievers, will they not say that you are out of your mind? But if all prophesy, and an unbeliever or an uninformed person comes in, he is convinced by all, he, he is convicted by all. (1 Corinthians 14:22–4)

The main difference between the gift of tongues and prophecy is that tongues are a sign to unbelievers: an indication to unbelievers of God's presence and power. Tongues will allow unbelievers to be convinced. The secrets of unbelievers are known, they are helped to refrain from them, and they will come and worship God. They will be able to witness the presence of God in His people.

If we speak in tongues and there is no interpretation for people to understand, to encourage us, then what is the purpose of speaking in tongues? What is spoken must have value, so that it will influence us to do Gospel work. Surely, this is the reason for going to church, not simply to hear people speaking in tongues. It is the Holy Spirit who allows people to speak in tongues. Any of us who speak this kind of language are born-again Christians and we are really in business with

God. It is surprising that many of us nowadays call ourselves prophets and speak in tongues. Sometimes we speak in tongues without even an interpretation, whereas the scriptures tell us that there should be an interpretation for any tongues spoken. Someone has to explain what is said, so that people can benefit from it.

Therefore, if the Bible is not wrong, what should those of us who speak in tongues without any interpretation be called? Are we Christians, or can speaking in tongues make us into born-again Christians? The Word of God must be with us before we can speak this language because it is authorised by the Holy Spirit. Only by doing the God's Word can we experience the presence of the Holy Spirit in our life, through speaking this language.

Prophesying is for those of us who believe. It is certain that those of us who prophesy, either by preaching or speaking, are known by God. The outcome of prophesying will be known publicly. Prophesying will let our secrets be exposed and enable us to come to God. Prophesying makes us born-again Christians. Prophecy is inspired by God, since we believe that Jesus Christ came to prophesy to the people as the Saviour, rather than speak in tongues. He prophesied to allow the people of God to understand His Gospel, its teachings and consequences.

Insight

Insight is wisdom and power from God. It is vital, because it lets us see deeply and understand people's problems. This is a gift of assistance, because it lets a problem be reviewed and examined, to gain a solution. Unfortunately, some of us use our privilege in order to condemn or spread whatever we see of other people. This misbehaviour holds back the demonstration of our gifts, causing a huge and damaging impact on the Gospel and to the people of God who have this gift.

Wisdom and knowledge

Wisdom is the act of demonstrating good judgement based on experience. It is given by God, and usually comes by applying knowledge from what we see, hear, read, and learn, since all these things influence our life. Knowledge is something that we know, and can be learned from people, books or papers. There are two main types of knowledge: natural knowledge and non-natural knowledge. The Bible states: *There are diversities of gifts, but the same Spirit. There are differences of activities, but it is the same God who works all in all. ...for to one is given the word of Wisdom through the spirit, to another the word of knowledge through the same Spirit. (1 Corinthians 12: 4–9)*

Natural knowledge comes from God and is given to humankind at birth. Observing or seeing things around us, we can experience this kind of knowledge. We all have this knowledge though our understanding of things around us. An example of this is the ability to differentiate between bad and good things. Non-natural knowledge is obtained by reading, teaching, advertising, and from others' advice. This type of knowledge is limited. Both types of knowledge have a huge effect on our lives, helping human kind in many areas. On the other hand, they can damage our life. The most important thing is that both types can work together to promote human life.

Wisdom and knowledge from God are also classified as natural and gospel wisdom and knowledge. Natural wisdom and knowledge are given to us by God, in order that we might be successful in life on this earth as well as in heaven, which is to come.

Gospel wisdom is a gift and is also known as words of wisdom. This gift enables us to examine God's mystery plan in different situations, and give advice and words of direction. It comes from God and from the application of knowledge of the Word of God. Gospel knowledge is also a gift, received from the Gospel. It comes by learning, reading or studying the Word of God. It is the skill of a person with words of assistance, or having wisdom and understanding into God's mystery in dealing with human beings, or with facts. The typical example of these kinds of gifts is King

Solomon in the Old Testament. Wisdom and knowledge can be received from other people, acquired through advice, teaching or reading.

There are two different outcomes, which at times depend on circumstances or our situations. However they are used, they will have an effect.

Effect of wisdom and knowledge

This is the result and the change in our life after applying them. We cannot use wisdom without applying knowledge. It is our responsibility to apply knowledge from birth, as well as knowledge we receive on this earth, and apply it well, to enable our wisdom to be effective, rather than our wisdom being dormant; this refers to inactive wisdom, and happens because of the wrong application of our knowledge and also a lack of understanding of human quality and talent. This quality refers to the image of God from which we human beings are created. The book of Genesis shows us that we were all created in the image of God.

God has the qualities that enable Him to be God of the universe and to do all things. The Lord has given us these qualities on this earth, so that we are able to fulfil His mission for us. Applying the knowledge and using the wisdom will let our qualities be discovered. However, it is strange to see that many of us always ask God to give us wisdom, while we do not know that we have it abundantly already. Also, we do not recognise that wisdom and knowledge are our resources, to achieve an efficient means of living, so we have to concentrate on them and use them in good ways. Others of us also ask God for more wisdom, without thinking of making use of our own natural knowledge. Even those of us who use our knowledge apply it wrongly because we do not examine the root of matters. Therefore, with all our wisdom and knowledge, we do not achieve what we expect in life. Good use of it may result in good outcomes and bad use in the opposite way. This has a huge impact on us and on others. Moreover, there are no specific ways of applying wisdom and knowledge, other than applying them in everyday life in all our doings.

The major areas influenced by the use of wisdom and knowledge are the growth of our wisdom and knowledge, and of our personal life both physical and spiritual. The application of this wisdom and knowledge is necessary and very important to us, since it has a huge impact on our life. It demonstrates our talent, performance and quality.

Interpretation of tongues

The *interpretation of tongues* is a message from God, an inspired utterance to explain the meaning of an unknown language. This is essential because the interpreter has to explain exactly what the other person has said, no matter what language has been spoken. In fact, we should know that the word from the interpreter is from God, even though someone spoke the language. Any of us in the church can interpret, but it should come from God rather than humans.

Miracles and healing

This is also a gift of the manifestation of God's power through us, to heal or to show a powerful manifestation of His power. The typical example from the Bible is shown in the book of *John 6: 1–13*, where five thousand people were fed.

The gift of healing deals with the deliverance of a person and physical salvation. This includes delivering somebody from sickness to health, or back to a normal condition. It is attributed to God's direct intervention through His servant, in a marvellous form, to show God's power and to bear witness to our own relationship with God, as well as that of the healer.

Faith

This is a spiritual gift and a manifestation of God's presence and power, which is freely given by God, for His glory and honour, and for service to His church. It is one of the demonstrations of power that enable us to believe in God and to call upon His power to do things without doubting.

It is one of the keys to the Gospel, and is based on our acceptance and our coming to Christ. There are many different reasons for us to do this. However, they are all to do with people's helpless situations. We may think that we have no protection or assistance from anybody apart from God; therefore, we decide to come to Christ for help in our areas of need. In fact, God cannot take care of these situations unless we have faith in God. Some of the areas of need are as follows: weakness, distress, sickness, homelessness, rejection, pleading for help, death and near-death.

Differences between the Holy Spirit and Spiritual Gifts

People might believe that the Holy Spirit is one of the gifts, but we all have this Spirit. God has given all of us this Spirit to overcome the spiritual powers, rulers and authority of this earth. The Holy Spirit is not the same as a spiritual gift. He is a comforter and mentor for us, and cannot be taken away from us. He replaces Jesus Christ, acting as the presence of the glory and power of God. We receive this right from the moment of our baptism. Although both the Holy Spirit and spiritual gifts do the same work of God, the Holy Spirit is purposely assigned for the Gospel, in order to save the lives of God's people. Gifts are not the same as the Holy Spirit, because God can take them away, since they are gifts from God.

Spiritual gifts area gift for individuals' needs, and therefore they are all different from each other. Like the Holy Spirit, gifts are some of the functions of the Word of God, given to us to save life, to proclaim the Gospel and to assist us in accomplishing our mission of the Gospel. They all work together to achieve the one ambition of the Gospel, which is to save people's lives.

5 The Church as a Marketplace

Jesus went into the temple and began to drive out those who bought and sold in the temple, and overturned the tables of the moneychangers and the seats of those who sold doves. And He would not allow anyone to carry wares through the temple. Then He taught, saying to them, "Is it not written, 'My house shall be called a house of prayer for all nations'? But you have made it a 'den of thieves.'" (Mark 11:15–17)

Introduction

What is a *marketplace* and, in particular, what does church as a marketplace mean?

In order for us to be effective and respond to the Gospel, a place for Gospel activities is needed. This is a church or kingdom hall; it is believed to be a holy place, because it is used for worshipping God or offering religious services to the Lord. The activities are provided by those of us who believe that God has given us gifts in Gospel teaching. These activities have a strong effect on the life of those present, because we believe that anything concerning the Gospel is from God.

The main response to the Gospel has two aspects: our relationship with God and our relationship with our neighbours and others. The outcome of our Christian life depends on the relationship between us and the activities. By combining these activities and Christianity in different ways, a variety of Christians can be seen in the same body of Christ.

This chapter shows that the church is God's present instrument or vehicle on earth, through which He desires to extend His Kingdom and fulfil His purpose. Therefore, it is described as *the pillar and ground of the truth (1 Timothy 3:15)*. Frederick. W. Robertson describes the church as that body of men in whom the spirit of God

116

dwells as the source of our excellence. The church is important for believers because of the Gospel, and therefore should not be used for any purpose other than the purpose of God to save people's lives

Church

The dictionary states that a church is a building for public Christian worship or religious services. It is also a group of people with the same religious beliefs and under the same authority and dominion. Some examples of these are the Presbyterian Church, the Methodist Church and the Charismatic Church.

The church refers to a body of people who have committed their lives to Jesus Christ to worship and follow him in obedience. According to *John 14:15–17*, it is the collective body of all of us who have God's Holy Spirit dwelling in our minds. Jesus Christ is the head of the church, and therefore a church belongs to the Lord.

The purpose of a church is to learn the word of God and put it into practice, in order to preach the true gospel to people as witnesses; it is also to make disciples of those whose minds God will open, to respond to the Gospel and to receive the gift of the Holy Spirit and the salvation of God. The power of the Holy Spirit is behind God's church, to enable it to witness to God the Creator.

However, the church is not only a building, as some of us think: it is us ourselves. It is this church that acts as an instrument to proclaim the Gospel. It is a public society for Christians who worship or offer religious services to the Lord: all of us who have been called out from darkness (the world) and have been separated for God. We have submitted and gathered together before God, in the name of Jesus Christ, for worship and fellowship, as stated in *1 Peter 2:4-10*. This tells us that God's own special people worship one Father, one Lord, and have one baptism and one faith. Our level of faith in God may be different, because of baby-, child- and adult-stages in our spiritual development as Christians.

Marketplace

In a *marketplace*, people buy and sell goods (such as fruit, clothes, shoes, food and meat) to get profit; a place where people trade in all kinds of things to make money. Stealing and cheating commonly take place, because buyers see goods at high prices, since, at times, some sellers wish to price their commodities high, to enable them to gain excessive profits.

The church as a marketplace refers to the way in which the church of God is used for other activities, as above in *Mark's* Gospel.

What is *a den of thieves?* Thieves are people who steal secretly or publicly. Most cases happen secretly, without applying force. Only people called armed robbers steal by attacking; at times, they can kill the victim, if someone opposes them. Thieves also take something from others in a way that the others do not have any clue about. They have wrong motives and ways to get something from others. Therefore, a den of thieves refers to a place where thieves have their headquarters, and is a place of liars. In the Gospel passage, Jesus tells His people that His house (the Temple) is full of thieves. Though we may call ourselves true Christians, inwardly we may not be. Some of us use God's house for wrong activities, in order to fulfil our personal ambitions, instead of using it for prayer. In fact, our God knows that it is going to happen, so he lets those of us who are determined to worship Him be aware of these people and their works, through the Gospel.

The church of God is now full of activities with the aim of getting money and property, and so the main purpose of the Church is out of hand. A question to ask ourselves is: how different is the church now from the marketplace, where people make money from businesses or do commerce to get money? Do we not use both places for the same ambition, which is money or personal achievement, instead of using it for worship or to offer religious services to the Lord?

For this, we have to know the meaning of Christianity. Christians have already been discussed earlier, but here are other details. It is a shame that the majority of us do not understand the meaning of Christianity and what it is all about. We think that only a small group of Christians in a particular church with familiar faces worshipping together are the only Christians. Therefore, apart from our church members or the few Christians we know, there are no Christians anywhere else.

My dear brethren in Christ, these raise a question to ask ourselves: what are Christians?

What are Christians?

As mentioned earlier, Christianity involves two things – our old nature and our new nature. We have turned away from our old nature towards God and have agreed to put away our old things that are bad. Since accepting the Lord, we have made up our mind to put away malpractice and put on good things.

We are not what some people think. We are followers of the Lord Jesus Christ; we belong to the religion of Christ, we believe in Christ and follow His teachings. We worship only one God, who is the Lord of Abraham, Isaac and Jacob. We fear this God and obey His Ten Commandments. We do what is right and are always willing to be more and more like the Lord Jesus Christ, to save people's lives through the doctrine of Jesus Christ.

We always seek God, trying to understand His Word deeply and put it into practice. We apply the Word of God in our life, so that God can make us fishers of men. Also, we believe that God's Word can do something for us, so we practise it at every moment. We always aim to apply the Word of God to our life, to allow the Holy Spirit to come in and enable us to fulfil our Christian mission.

Any of us are Christians if we have accepted Jesus Christ of Nazareth as our personal Saviour, and worship Him as the Highest

God, truly and with commitment.

We are told that there is one body but many members (*1 Corinthians 12:12*). So we are not only in one church of God, neither are we confined to one place, as most of us think. Rather, all members of the church of God are Christians and we are all over the whole world.

If we say worship God, it does not necessarily mean that if we go to church or do church activities all the time, we are worshipping God. Worship means applying God's Word to have an impact on our life. Thus, the change in our life can be seen by people around, enabling them to come and worship the same God.

A further question: is the God of Abraham, Isaac and Jacob in one temple or church? No, God is not only in one temple or church – He is in all His churches. The church is God's present instrument on earth, through which He desires to extend His Kingdom and fulfil His purpose. Since some of us do not understand the meaning of church, what Christians are and what we are supposed to be, we abuse the Gospel.

My Own Experience

I remember when my wife Elly and I married. I am a Charismatic member and my beloved wife is a Presbyterian member. It was very sad and surprising to hear some questions from some so-called born-again Christians, such as, "Isaac, I have heard that your wife is a Presbyterian!" Their implication was that my wife is not a Christian, since she is a Presbyterian member; if she is, she is not recognised or there is something wrong with her being a Presbyterian.
They went even further and asked her "Are you Isaac's wife?"

My wife, filled with the Holy Spirit, responded, "Yes, I am. Is the Presbyterian Church not a church of God? Are members of Presbyterian churches not Christians? Do we not use the same Bible as other churches of God? Is the God of Presbyterian churches different from the God of Charismatic and other churches? Also, is the Lord interested in our church differences, or our commitment to follow in His footsteps?"

Most of us believers are churchgoers or church spectators. We do not always know and understand what church means, as well as being Christians, our reasons for going to church and its importance. It is essential for all of us to understand these basic things, because it is the root of calling ourselves Christians. If the clear understanding of these basic Gospel foundations is lacking, we may be in the church for many years without growth. We will not see the need to be committed to one church and to be actively involved in that specific church of God. Also, we will not develop and become mature in personal growth and will not find full realisation in the ministry that God has given us.

It is also very common these days for many of the so-called born-again Christians to move from one church to another, because of increasing problems they encounter. These believers are regarded as true followers of God, but move from one church to another, day in and day out. They are flying like butterflies. Why? Is not Jesus Christ of Nazareth the head of all His churches? Some of their attitudes and behaviours are contrary to the disciples of Christ and they are not prepared to refrain from them. It is hardly thinkable that these people understand the message of our Lord Jesus Christ. Therefore, a question arises here: does this all influence our lives or that of other believers? If yes, how and when are these problems going to be solved, to enable others to achieve their vision?

Some of these problems are because of their immaturity in personal growth in the Word of God. Most of us are still in the world because we are not yet well grounded in the Word of Life. It would be very difficult to come out with positive assurances that all these problems will be overcome within a short time, since we create most of the problems ourselves, and as a result, we have to solve them. We can do this only if we are well trained by the Word of God, and we focus on our Lord and forget the things of the world. However, unfortunately we prefer the things of the world to taking up the cross of our Lord, because of personal achievements.

Furthermore, the solution to these problems has indeed to do with our Lord's grace, since most of them are Satan's activities, designed to cause confusion in God's Kingdom, to persuade believers to give in to the world, and also to destroy the entire body of Christ. As a consequence, we believers in Christ have to cling to our Lord and focus on Him in all situations with our heart, our commitment and our prayers. We need to stop moving from one church to another, because most of the problems are the work of the devil. It is not surprising to hear that the body of Christ is full of Satan's agents. They are increasing the body of Christ by joining it, with their ambition to destroy it and to get members, since the world is coming to an end as the Second Coming of the King of kings approaches.

On the other hand, if we move from church to church because of our brothers' and sisters' attitudes and behaviours, then what are we? Are we religious, or Christian? We should not move from one church to another, no matter what happens to us or what we may go through. At times, it may not be easy to cope with some things, but we have to keep our fingers crossed and resist any programme or affair that will cause damage to the Gospel and to the children of God. We believers have a motto: 'God is in control!' Is this true or false? We have to know and believe that, whatever happens, our Maker is in control. However, the Lord in control does not mean that we can sit back unconcerned, and let malpractice happen in the church. We have to be strong and continue to point out things that are going on in God's Kingdom which are contrary to the Gospel, until the problems are solved completely. By doing this, we will show the type of Christians we are.

It is strange that we Christians do not like comments and disagreements. Why? Are we perfect to the extent that whatever we do or say is absolutely right? Even the Lord Jesus Christ himself was criticised. People made comments and disagreed with what He did since they did not understand some of His teachings or believed in what He did. Jesus did not ignore them, but He explained things to them.

The Word of God tells us that nobody is perfect. So we must ask ourselves: is the Book of Life wrong? Having disagreements helps us learn more from each other and correct our mistakes. It helps us make right decisions and to help ourselves and help people who are suffering, as well as do missionary work. We must realise that it is our God, not human beings, who calls us to His ministry. He calls us for a purpose, and not to be in His Kingdom as spectators. Rather, He calls us into His Kingdom as missionaries to the world, to convert people in the darkness to His Gospel. What would be the outcome of our calling into the Kingdom of God if we sit back and let malpractice happen in the Kingdom?

Therefore, our Maker in control means that the Lord's power can break every chain and continues to give us life and victory always in every situation, if we trust in His Word, Cross, Blood and His Name. Everything will be successful if we do the right thing in the right place. Indeed, being Christians is about hearing God's Word and doing it, which allows us to become followers. However, if we hear the Word and do not follow it, how can we be called followers of God?

Aim of a Church

An *aim* is something that a person has in mind to obtain or do. It is essential in our life, since it plays a major part in success and failure. Achieving our aim can never be successful without a plan.

The *aim of a church* means the use of a church of God, which in particular is *a house of prayer for all nations (Mark 11:17)*. It is the means by which God achieves His purpose for His children. This purpose is to extend His Kingdom, to save His children's lives from darkness. The Lord's goal was to be a good Messiah to humankind. So, in order to achieve this aim, He had to have a plan, which is the Church. Therefore, His church has to be established, as a means of bringing His children from the bondage of sin to be saved and to fulfil His purpose.

Jesus went into the temple and began to drive out those who bought and sold in the temple, and overturned the tables of the moneychangers and the seats of those who sold doves. And He would not allow anyone to carry wares through the temple. Then He taught, saying to them, "Is it not written, 'My house shall be called a house of prayer for all nations'? But you have made it a 'den of thieves.'"(Mark 11:15–17)

5.1: Jesus Christ cleanses the Temple

However, the children of God use the house of God as a market place for buying and selling, for our own personal achievements. The Bible tells us that a similar thing happened during the time of the Lord Jesus Christ of Nazareth. When Christ noticed that people were buying and selling (see picture), He was really angry and cleansed the Temple of God. The Lord seriously said that the people were carrying out commerce, and that the house of God was meant for prayer instead of commerce. Do we know why Jesus Christ was so angry? Jesus Christ was very upset because people were buying and selling their goods there, rather than using it for prayer and worship. These sellers were selling sheep, bulls and doves at very high prices to those who needed them, in order to make a profit. Truly, they were cheating the people to make money to achieve their personal ambitions.

Firstly, the sellers should not have been selling in the Temple at all, since the Temple was not meant to be a marketplace. Secondly, they were trying to make more money from the people who were in need and had come to the Temple for assistance. Thirdly, they were using the Temple to steal and to cheat people. Certainly, they were concerned with their own needs, rather than with the Gospel. This greatly annoyed Jesus Christ, so He overturned all the tables of the moneychangers and scattered their money, and drove the animals out of the Temple, telling the sellers to stop using His Father's house as a place for making money.

We Christians have to ask ourselves whether this is different from what some of us are doing in the church of God today. We may not trade in the same sheep, bulls and doves these days to obtain money and property, as the sellers were trading in the Temple. However, we are using the name of the Lord to influence the disciples of the Lord as well as the public, for our own personal ambitions. What are we, who call ourselves born-again and Spirit-filled Christians, doing now, different from what people did in the past? Jesus drove away the people who were buying and selling in the Temple, because He knew that if the house of God, which is the Christians' 'filling station' is polluted, then we are seriously in trouble. It will hinder the manifestation of the gifts and the fruit of the Holy Spirit in us.

Thus, when Jesus Christ saw this happening, He destroyed all the sellers' goods without mercy. Unfortunately, we are doing the same things as the people then. Instead of using the church of God for prayer, as our Maker asked us to do, we are using it to make money for ourselves and to achieve our ambitions.

We must be led into a deeper experience of the Holy Spirit and His power. To be able to do this, we must set aside all physical matters and set some days of prayer for ourselves, for unbelievers and backsliders, to enter into the Kingdom of God and its ministries. We have to renew everything, and this begins with prayer. We can only go forward with a wholehearted commitment to changes, not only in prayer, but also in our behaviour and attitudes as the children of God. Coming to church to worship God has to be of major importance to all of us born-again Christians. It has to be this, and not the feeling of love and acceptance from the congregation, or using the Lord's church as a marketplace for buying and selling, in order to get profit for our own affairs.

This issue has moved the Holy Spirit away from us, and now we are empty. There is no power, joy or life in us. The gifts and grace of the Holy Spirit must be seen in a growing, witnessing church in this century, which must make an impact on the world around. If we are not experiencing this, then the church should not aim to be called Charismatic.

Do we know the reasons why Jesus drove away the people who were using God's house as a market instead of prayer? Do we know the implication of not using the church of God as a marketplace, but rather for prayer, as the Lord said? Do we fully understand it? Or are we concentrating on the physical world, instead of looking for spiritual things?

Jesus Christ of Nazareth knew that using the house of the Lord for something else instead of for prayer would drive away the power of God from us. This is because God is holy and everything is holy. The Holy Spirit, who is our comforter, guard and our everything, is also holy. We receive power from our Father through this Holy Spirit. So, if we are not cleansed, or if where we dwell is unclean, then the Holy Spirit cannot come to us or to our unclean place. As a result, there will be no link between the Holy Spirit and us. We have to ask ourselves how we can expect God to bless us if we are not cleansed, when there is no peace, joy and life. We must be involved in the renewal fully, so that the renewal movement will have something to give to each and every one of us. Are we ready to tackle such a problem? We have to know that our God is always very much around; therefore, we will be able to solve any problem if we are willing to do so.

At this point we have to understand what the marketplace is about and the aim of marketing, as Jesus experienced in the Book of Life.

Aim of a Market

The main *aim of a market* is to achieve profit and not loss.

We have to understand the Bible and all that Jesus said and did. Jesus constantly talked in parables. He did not compare the house of God to a physical marketplace where buying and selling take place in order to get profit. Jesus said His Father's house is for prayer and not a marketplace! It is not a place for us to do business, in order to gain profit or to obtain our personal achievements. This statement tells us that we have to devote ourselves to spiritual things rather than worldly things. Also, Jesus asks us to use His church for prayer, because prayer is the life and soul of spirituality, instead of using it for the things of the world.

Jesus Christ refers to the house of God as a place where Christians' hearts are, a place where His disciples' spiritual lives dwell. This is why, when He saw people buying and selling, it upset Him so much, to the extent that He destroyed all the sellers' goods, without having mercy on them. He knew that the church is the 'filling station' of the Gospel. It is the place where we go and fill up with 'fuel'. We all need fuel (the Word of God) to sustain us in this world, as vehicles need fuel or petrol to work.

So, if this fuel is polluted, or the filling-station of the Gospel is destroyed, what will happen?

Unfortunately, some of us are doing the same thing in the church of God. As a result, we are denying our Lord Jesus Christ, abusing Christianity, and cursing ourselves. People are using the name of the Lord to influence other Christians or the public, to make money or obtain our personal achievements. In fact, through this disobedience, we encounter numerous problems in the Kingdom of God now, and these problems cause huge damage to Christianity and to disciples of Christ.

Church Problems

Problems are things that cause difficulties. Problems always prolong matters, and at times they put people off their tasks, normally resulting in doubt. Anyone who faces problems feels uncomfortable at that particular time. Every problem has a cause. It can destroy us and even end our life, since problems that have an impact on our life are the main issue to solve. There are many kinds of problems that we experience in our everyday life; for example, problems to do with wealth, relationships and social conduct.

Church problems are difficulties that we face in the Kingdom of God, either because of wrong activities or situations. These are the unacceptable service and character of some of us. The church has become a ground for dominion. This is because there are many activities and malpractices that have these sorts of problems; however, our concerns are not welcomed. This means that only a few people in the church can say anything about what goes on or express our opinions. It is very sad and unfair that we are not given a real opportunity to put across our views about things that go on in the church of God. Since we bother about our future, it is very important for us to come out and express our opinion and concerns.

On the other hand, others of us are not concerned about these malpractices, because we think that it is up to God to take action on these issues, and because we do not feel passionately about the matters, since we do not have a clue about our development and the church. Truly, we need know and understand that success in our existence and in our everlasting life depends on worshipping sincerely. This will come directly from our involvement in the Gospel of Christ. Then we will feel passionately and take action about these malpractices, to let the church of Christ move on to its destination.

The body of Christ is an association or institution, which is under a dictatorship of people instead of God. It is under a dictatorship because a few people rule God's church and only these people have a say in it and can express their concerns. However, looking at the Gospel of Christ, we all have a vital role in keeping the church, which cannot move on without the expression of our opinions about what goes on in the church. We should not be under a dictatorship. We are definitely not protected from dictatorship in the Gospel. All these problems in the body of Christ have a damging effect on the Gospel.

We are concerned about our development, both physical and spiritual; however, we often do not realise that malpractice has a huge influence on this issue. We do not realise how some Christians are using God's Name and His properties in any ways they choose; this influences the Gospel's reputation and also lets the public underestimate us. Seriously, the church is a place for God's worship, for prayer and services to God, and nothing else. In fact, it is not the place for the worship of people, and neither is it a commercial place, nor a place for all sorts of tricks to obtain personal ambition or achievements. Because of these different purposes that churches of God are being used for, instead of worshipping God, the houses of God are full of problems. These difficulties that we experience in the body of Christ constantly influence the physical and spiritual aspects of our life, as well as the entire development of the Christian ministry.

These problems prevent us recognising our need of Jesus' blood and our need to link with each other to support ourselves. It has even become hard to build up cohesive friendships with members in the same body, because there is no love and trust. Conversely, we sometimes depend on the people in the church rather than God, thinking that these people will help our needs. This is because we do not know the importance of the Gospel in our lives, focusing on the Word of God, to enable us to be equipped and developed in the social and spiritual aspects of our everyday life. It will also allow us to experience Gospel benefits, in order to proclaim the Gospel to save the lives of people around the world.

Below are the main problems of using the church of God as a marketplace:
- Poverty
- Sickness and disease
- Lack of power and authority
- Decline of church membership
- Difficulties in evangelism and witness
- No powerful testimonies
- No spiritual growth
- Lack of spiritual gifts
- Weddings – wrong ones and high costs
- False religions and false Christians
- Fornication and adultery

- False religion
- Treating people differently
- Selfishness and wrong self-esteem
- Envy

Poverty

Poverty is a state of being poor. People are poor when they own nothing at all, or when they do not have enough money for food, water, clothes and shelter that are the necessities of life. Common reasons are sickness and war. When someone is so severely sick that they are out of work, this can cause their poverty. If a country is at war, this can cause the citizens of that country to become poor. Even those people who are rich can become poor or might be reduced from wealth to poverty because of war. Poverty puts human kind in poor health and it even kills. This kind of poverty is one of the main causes of the church of God being used as a marketplace. Thus, God's church is being used for commerce or commercial reasons to obtain money and property, instead of prayer and other purposes of the Gospel in order to save people's lives.

Sickness and disease

Sickness and disease describe the condition of Christians now. Many of us are in a bad condition in the body of Christ: sickness, poor health and discomfort. Even those of us who are well always look sick. We do not feel happy in our lives, so we are characterised by sickness every day. In fact, the Bible states that the death of Jesus Christ on the cross brought all our woes to an end, so we have victory over everything. By His stripes, we are healed. Still the house of the Lord is full of sickness and disease. All the time, we engage in our problems rather than disengaging from them. This is because we are using God's house as a marketplace for our personal achievements, instead of prayer and worshipping the Lord! This drives the power of God away from us. It also holds back our victory on the cross by Christ, so sickness and disease as well as poverty are now common in the Kingdom of God.

We now add whatever we want to the basis of Christianity, or omit from it what we do not like, as suits us. We do all sorts of these things to win members into 'our churches', as we think of them. The main purpose of this is to obtain our own achievements. It is vitally important for us to understand that we cannot add anything to the basis of Christianity, or omit anything from it; neither can we do anything to change God. Some of us outwardly regard church as God's church, while inwardly we do not. We just use the name of God to achieve our ambition, since we understand that it is only by doing this that we can be successful. This has driven away from us the authority given to us at the cross of Calvary, and has replaced it with all types of woes.

So, if we want to get away from these woes, and experience the authority given to us at the cross of Calvary and boast that we are the true disciples of Christ, then we have to fear God, keep His Word and obey it.

Lack of power and authority

Power is the ability to do things. It is one of the main tools to demonstrate the kind of God we worship. It allows us, as well as the public, to acknowledge God as the true and highest God. The manifestation of power usually makes the work of the Gospel easier and more interesting.

With *authority*, the right power to control everything on this earth is given to all of us by God. It is the same as parents having authority over their children. This legal authority to overcome God's creatures was caused by the blood of Christ on the Cross of Calvary and His resurrection. This authority allows us to perform things ourselves on behalf of God and allows the Gospel to be authentic.

Lack of power and authority means our incapacity to use our position and the Word of God to control the world's goods, or to do things in order to promote the Gospel. The things are wealth, property or belongings, that influence our goodness and the Gospel tasks assigned by God to us. These are some examples of means to spread the Gospel to save people's lives and an entire breakthrough in our life. The Bible assures us that, with faith in the Lord, which is the Word of God, the deaf will hear, the blind see and the lame dance. All these promises do not seem to happen as they are supposed to.

It is very hard for us to cope with the world-situation now, because of this lack of power and authority. The weakness of our authority and power are shattering the wonderful work that God has done for His people. It is such a pity that God has offered His good office to us in good faith, which is His followers continuing His work. We are messing things up; we constantly try to look good in public and be seen as good-hearted, but we are considered as good for nothing so far as the work of God is concerned. As Christians, we have to be determined to do God's work faithfully, so that our goodness and care will show to others that we are disciples of Christ. Our goodness must be demonstrated by the many good deeds we do, so that our lives will have an impact on others' lives. Our ability to do all these things depends on our understanding of the Word of God and the power and authority that we are aware of possessing through Christ.

The main root of this problem of the lack of power and authority is that we still do not understand the things of God, since we have not received a new life, which is the life of Christ, even though we are in the position of being Christians. This means that we do Gospel work, but are not willing to change our old life and put on God's life. We are still the same as we were before we came to Christ. We do all sorts of things that are contrary to the Word of God, as if we are in the past. We publicly and boldly proclaim ourselves to be Christians. However, this is not the case, for inwardly we are totally different. This disobedience and hypocrisy have driven away the authority given to us to perform things in order to prove the Gospel. We are very weak in all aspects of life, since we lack this power. It makes our work very difficult. The lack of this power has become a problem for us and it causes a huge downfall for us.

Decline of church membership

The level of followers of Christ is falling day in and day out. We experience declining membership instead of constant growth. Here are some of the common reasons for this: the attitude of fellow-Christians, and Christians' disagreement about the misuse of the church.

It seems that we are hungry for the Gospel. We go to church to worship our Maker. However, it is the same Christians who move from church to church, since perhaps they do not experience what they want. This movement may at times result in backsliding, if we feel that nothing is happening in our life. In fact, as the proverb states, 'seeing is believing'. As Christians, we must witness to God's presence all the time in both physical and spiritual ways, to strengthen us always in our focus on God.

Most non-Christians who come to Christ backslide, as a result of problems in the body of Christ. It also happens because of the great expectation that new Christians have about disciples of Christ.

Difficulties in evangelism and witness

Evangelism is Christianity's presentation to the public or to the people of God, with the goal of letting them have faith in the Lord, to enable them to come and worship Him. A *witness* is anyone who bears witness to the truths about God and His Gospel; witnesses certainly believe that they have been called to do this. Both evangelism and witness have the same goal. The goal is to bring the world's people to Christ, so that God will save their lives. Evangelism and witness are certainly based on the power of God; it is the Holy Spirit who brings people in darkness to Christ. However, we as Christians do the physical aspect of it, since our character and attitudes convince most people of the Word, before they decide to accept Christ. It is necessary for us to do the work of God, before we can go out to spread the good news.

When we accept Jesus Christ as our personal Saviour through baptism, we believe that Jesus Christ washes all our sins away.

Because of this, we are supposed to put on good things in order to be like God, since we have become new creatures. It is this new life that enables us to spread the Word of God. At the same time, it is this issue of new and improving life that we aim at all the time that will allow God to use us. We can also develop this through the Word of God feeding us at church and our efforts in studying it.

No powerful testimonies

A *testimony* is an account of what God has done for us; it is an act of praise and worship; it is another way of thanking God for what He has done for us. It always reminds us what God has done for us. There are many types of testimonies of God, such as healing the sick, providing for or protecting them. Testimonies are different from each other, and this usually depends on our differing circumstances.

The issue of no powerful testimonies means that our testimonies now do not influence people's everyday lives. Testimonies demonstrate the presence, love and power of God, which encourage us to focus on the Gospel. So, whatever the testimony, it has some aspects to have an impact on our life. In fact, we can have many testimonies, which is fine. However, the most important thing about having a testimony is to have an effect. We need God every moment; we have to be taught and led by God, so that we too will be able to teach others and lead them to God. If we are not taught and led by God, how we can teach others and lead them to God, especially those who are in the world? We should know what God has done for us, in order to give thanks to God. We should have a story to tell and a song to sing, and it is through this testimony we will be enabled to do that. It shows us that God can decrease the power of temptation by the devil, and assure us that we need God all the time. We show appreciation to God for what He has done for us, in all His marvellous works. Having a testimony is one of the things that can help us do that. Testimony is carried out by God to show His truth, His nature and the importance of His Gospel. Therefore, it would be a great help for us to have a sound testimony, because it will allow us to understand the effectiveness of the Word of God. Testimonies offer regular support, and help us develop and improve our Christianity. These testimonies act as feedback, and remind us of the love and care of God and His ability to do all things.

The aim of testimonies is to provide support and assistance to those suffering, and to improve the condition of their life. Testimony is a sign of assurance by God to His children for the future, so testimonies with no effect on people's life because of malpractice in the church will do no good to humankind.

No spiritual growth

Spiritual growth is the most important thing in our life. Our spirit has to grow, to enable us to go forth and tell, to equip us for ministry, to preach the Word of Life effectively and efficiently, and also to give us hope for the future. It is really difficult to know who are genuine Christians. As the world is coming to an end, so do we face many problems, even in the body of Christ. It takes only those believers whose spirit has grown. Our growing spirit will enable us to know whether a person, prophet or message is from God. Our spirit is not growing as it should, because of our malpractice. We use the house of God to obtain our wishes, instead of using it for prayer and God's service. We take God's church as our own property and do whatever we wish. This influences the relationship between us and the Holy Spirit, and so we face many problems.

The Holy Spirit is our helper and comforter, interacting between us and God. He comforts us and helps us overcome our problems. He also helps us release our minds from sin, and helps us concentrate on God and continue to worship Him. We cannot experience God's presence and His power without the Holy Spirit. Because of malpractice, our spirit is not growing to enable us to work like the Lord Jesus Christ. Since our spirit is not growing, we are not strong enough to stand against the things of this world. So we are always confused about God's worship and blessings, because we do not experience anything to help us develop.

Lack of spiritual gifts

Spiritual gifts deal with the spirit or soul. They are given freely to us by God, to express friendship or the relationship between us and God. They are some of the functions of the Word of God given to us to save life, to proclaim the Gospel and to help us accomplish our mission of the Gospel.

There are many spiritual gifts to which we are all entitled. Some of them are: the gift of tongues, of prophecy, of wisdom and knowledge, of the interpretation of tongues, of miracles and of healing. They are all different, but all work together to achieve the one ambition of the Gospel, which is to save people's lives. They are given to all of us, so that we can experience the presence and power of God, and continue our enjoyment of the Gospel. They help us focus on the Gospel if there are temptations and problems.

The lack of spiritual gifts refers to what we do not experience. It indicates that we are not worshipping God intimately, and that we are taking the worship of God lightly. Put simply, we do not understand deeply what the Gospel is. We think that we just become Christians, and that is all. Therefore, as long as we are Christians, going to church regularly and participating in church activities, without concentrating on the Word of God that will change us for the better, we have nothing to do again. We always put effort into worshipping God, but these efforts are not effective. The Lord has given us power, authority, wisdom and knowledge freely to be used; for all that, we do not make use of them.

This lack of spiritual gifts in the body of Christ is threatening our lives. Many of us are sick, poor and have problems, but there is no solution. For example, nobody has any idea how sick people are going to be healed or treated, or how people's problems are to be solved. In fact, there is no commitment to take care of each other. The church of God is not under any obligation to take responsibility for other people, even in terms of sickness. Truly, we are now experiencing many problems in our lives. It seems as if there is no God. We are desperate and shift around all the time, because we think that nobody cares about us. There is no help from anywhere, since the problems of the world weigh us down when we do the work of God. This is all because we do not experience the spiritual gifts; doubt has become part of our lives. Doubt has let us forget that the Spirit of God is with us at every moment, always moving over us. We forget that of course there will be trials and temptations. It is during this time that we have to stand up to whatever happens to us, believing that our God will never fail or forsake us. We are the 'fruits of the Gospel of Christ'. We have now become the main tree producing the fruits, instead of being the fruits produced by the tree, which is the Gospel. We take the Gospel into our own hands and do whatever we want.

Weddings – wrong ones and high costs

When something is *wrong*, it is not what it should be, or something is done contrary to the facts. Doing wrong is part of our human life; we are all bound to do wrong or make a mistake, because it is in our nature. However, it is better for us to do right things all the time. Therefore, it would be a credit if our lives could be bound up with right or good doings. Doing wrong things to others can cause them harm, so it is advisable for everyone to avoid from wrongdoing. People who do wrong all the time can be considered to be evil people, even though they may not possess an evil spirit.

Wrong weddings are the weddings of Christians without the consent of our parents or families. Some of us get married while our parents or families have no clue about the marriage; others of us get married without the traditional marriage rite. People's family may be taken to include both members and ancestors. In our family, we relate to each other as one body, and we demonstrate love and care for others. We are the people who, from their childhood, take care of those who now want to get married. We are committed to helping, protecting and supporting them, right from their infancy. We take responsibility for them, give advice and assistance, and we use our wealth to raise and support them. We are the people who offer support and personal development for them, in order that they should be successful in life in the future.

Some of us get married without letting family know about it. As Christians, is it right to get married without informing our family or parents? Or is it right to get married by ignoring the traditional marriage rite? Truly, it is totally wrong to do this, because it does not follow the Ten Commandments. The Ten Commandments are the laws that God gave to Moses for His children to follow. They are rules for living and for worshipping God. It goes against the commandment, *Honour your father and your mother, that your days may be long upon the land which the Lord your God is giving you (Exodus 20:12)*. Can we get married by having just a wedding? Surely, it seems that we do not know the ideal and importance of the family behind the marriage, neither have we understood the role of marriage in the Gospel of Christ.

This marriage ignorance makes our conception of a wedding different from the Biblical requirements of marriage. Our behaviour is influencing people's high regard of the entire body of Christ and of Christianity.

On the other hand, some of us enter into marriage with our own personal purposes. We want to get married with the aim of obtaining something from the other partner, or using them to obtain our wishes. By practising such things, we lead our marriage onto the rocks in the future, since we are acting totally against the ideals of getting married. All these things cause many problems, such as marital breakdown, which is a big affliction to the Gospel of Christ.

High wedding costs are the huge amount of money spent on the wedding. This amount of money beforehand is too high, to the extent that we find it hard to afford. This causes tremendously high expectations of our weddings. We follow the world and do the same thing, instead of focusing on the Lord. We do not know the role of marriage in Christianity, so we are not interested in the married couple's relationship, but we are very interested in worldly affairs, like the money spent on our weddings. The high cost of weddings causes many problems in the kingdom of God, such as debt, sexual immorality and even marriage breakdown that have a huge impact on us and on the Gospel. The Gospels proclaim that Jesus knew about marriage, and the vital role it plays in Christianity.

Because of these high wedding costs, divorce is increasing. We want to have wonderful weddings to glorify our Lord's name, without considering our situation or circumstances. We do not assess the cost involved and its significance before we proceed. In fact, we are ignoring the Word of God and are doing our own thing. Since we do not depend on God, our wedding expectations result in problems for the married couples, such as huge debt. This creates numerous problems that contribute to the high rate of Christian marital separation that is both incredible and very concerning.

Debt is the money owed to somebody or to the bank. The debt comes because of money given to a person by another person or a bank. This loan usually acts as first aid, because it helps people to get out of their immediate problems. However, the loan does us no good, since it always makes the situation worse. We look at other sources for financial help, if we think we do not have enough money to cater for what we want and consider important in life. We do this without considering the future situation beforehand.

The high cost of Christian weddings causes debt for married couples and creates many problems. The majority of us take a loan with interest from many sources to pay for our weddings, with the aim of paying back later. Having borrowed the money for the wedding, paying off the loan becomes a big problem for the couple to bear. Since the loan may be a huge amount with interest to pay also, it can never be repaid in a short period of time. As a result, it causes many problems in the marriage and it can contribute to their failing.

The high cost of weddings now causes increasing *sexual immorality* in the body of Christ, since it prolongs the time before Christian marriages, and this influences our development as Christians and the development of God's church. The time we take to get married does not help the Gospel. In fact, timing is essential in our life.

When Christian weddings are compared to other weddings, for example traditional ones, the latter is simple and its cost is lower than Christian weddings, so those who believe in customary weddings can afford to do them quickly. The families of the partners, especially the woman's family, believe that the relationship between their daughter and the man is more important thing than anything else. Therefore, we see that the man who is coming to marry our daughter can afford whatever is in accordance with our customary rites. It does not matter whether the woman comes from our family or not. The woman's family refuses to make things difficult for the man and his family. We are always willing to give our beautiful and precious daughter away to marry a man who will come to us and ask for our daughter, provided she loves the man. All the arrangements and procedures are made quickly for a customary wedding, since the woman's family make things easier for the man. This avoids the problem of sexual immorality of the partners about to get married. However, Christian weddings are totally different, because without much money, you cannot get married. This implies that those of who are single and poor are not going to get married. So, it is hard for us to get married, and when we do, the costs are high. The ensuing sexual immorality is now influencing the entire body of Christ.

False religions and false Christians

False religions concern those who believe in other gods but use the name of the Lord Jesus Christ to enable them to accomplish their ambitions. They connect to God's churches to confuse Christian followers and make them follow these leaders. They confuse us by saying that we all believe in the same God, but participate in religion in different ways or on different days. If we study their religious teachings and worship in detail, we can see that they worship different gods. They publicly classify themselves as Christians and followers of Jesus Christ, whereas that is not the case.

We must ask ourselves if God approves of all religions. Honestly, God does not approve of all religions. The Bible tells us that there will be many false Christians and prophets who will publicly declare that they know God, but inwardly they do not. These people disown God by their works. There are many religious people now who pretend that they are disciples of Jesus Christ of Nazareth, but their attitudes and behaviour are contrary to what is required of them. Their religious attitudes and rites of worship display confusion and distortion, showing that they are not followers of Jesus Christ. These peoples use the names of God to commit crime, cheat, and steal from people. They break marriages and split families. They have no doubt that what they do in the name of God is right and approved by God in the Book of Life.

We must be very careful in all situations, because all these people have a bad influence on our lives, as well as destroying the entire body of Christ. We know that time and the world will pass away, and that God's Word shall endure forever. Furthermore, God searches our hearts and minds, and gives to each one of us according to our works.

False Christians are people of God in the body of Christ who seem to be real followers of Christ, while inwardly they are not. They come into God's churches for their own purposes. These Christians cheat, deceive and do all sorts of tricks, so that they can fulfil their ambitions. They are counterfeit Christians, as God assures us. They are devoted to the Christian religion, and participate in and organise activities. It looks as if they are more interested in worshipping God than any others of us. Such Christians proclaim that they have experienced the religion of the Lord Jesus Christ and that their Christianity is outstanding. These days, there are so many of these dishonest Christians such as prophets, pastors and their followers in the Kingdom of God. We must ask ourselves why this is. Prophets and pastors are supposed to proclaim a message committing us to one another. They pass on the message given to them by God. It is very surprising that most of the modern prophets and pastors pervert the message of the Bible. The words of the living God are intentionally being changed all the time. By this, people are in different ways doing things to suit themselves or the public or congregations, for their own achievements. They do this instead of bringing the whole true message for our life, relating it to social, moral and cultural as well as personal issues, which is the most vital thing for us.

Also, an amazing thing is that these people, who seem to be born-again and spirit-filled Christians, influence people to come and join their churches, by saying negative things about other churches of God. Their ideas about other churches make the public ill and have a bad influence on our life. Moreover, these people deny Jesus Christ and damage the entire body of Christ with their attitudes and behaviour. This makes it very difficult for us to focus on the Lord and use our influence to persuade people to come and join the body of Christ. We must ask ourselves if these people are real followers of Christ!

There are many incidents in the Gospels of false prophets; they claim to be prophets of God and yet are not. *Matthew 7:15, 24:11, Mark 13:22, Luke 6:26*

Revelation 19:20 refers to the last times, during which there will be false prophets, who will eventually be thrown into the lake of fire.

My brothers and sisters in Christ, there are so many false prophets, pastors and followers in the body of Christ now, who use the name of the Lord in vain, as the Bible tells us. They pretend to be true disciples of the Lord. They fight for members or other church-members to join them in their church, for money. These people use God's name to get personal property, and for their personal ambitions. They use God's name in vain, to cheat and steal from people and the Kingdom of God, instead of teaching the Good News. Their religious rites and attitudes of worship, as well as their character and Christian lives show confusion and distortion, and show that they are chasing the things of the world rather than the things of Heaven. The Bible tells us to devote ourselves to spiritual things instead of worldly things. It is very surprising that some of these people, who teach the Gospel of Christ, refuse to do this, and continue to chase things of the world. It is a reasonable belief that these people are not real followers of Jesus Christ. Therefore, we must be very careful not to believe every spirit, as the Bible warns us about these false people.

Again, a question to ask ourselves is whether Jesus Christ's warning about false prophets means that all prophets and pastors in the body of Christ are false people. Evidently it does not mean this. A very difficult problem that arises here is how to know true or false prophets and pastors, since all use God's name in their activities. Do we believe that those who speak lies in the name of the Lord will not live? We must know that there will be a day when liars will be ashamed of their visions and prophecies. Believers in Christ, the great day of God is coming, burning like an oven. Are we preparing to repent of our wrong doings before the Lord and ask for forgiveness before the time comes, or we will still give in to self and Satan?

May our Lord and Maker come to our souls through the Gospel speaking and let His words, His cross and His crown lighten all our seeking. Also, may He drive out the darkness from our hearts and plant in every inward part truthfulness and kindness.

Effects of false religions and false Christians

The effects are that they:
- damage the entire body of Jesus Christ
- discourage believers and do not lead to spiritual growth
- confuse unbelievers
- drive away the power of God from us
- hold back our victory through the cross
- reduce the numbers of disciples of Christ.

Fornication and adultery

Fornication is simply sexual intercourse between unmarried people, which is a symbol for idolatry and harlotry against God. *Adultery* is sexual intercourse between a married person and an unmarried person, or between two people who are married to others.. Now the house of the Lord is full of fornication and adultery, because of the temporary things of this world such as money, property and achievements. These temporary things force so many Christians to turn away from the Lord our Maker. The Bible mentions these, among other sins: *out of the heart proceed evil thoughts, murders, adulteries, fornications, thefts, false witness, blasphemies. These are the things which defile a man. (Matthew 15: 19–20)*

As seen before, the costs of Christian weddings also contribute to the problem of fornication in the body of Christ. If this happens, some people become frustrated and forget about marriage. Sometimes, we are more interested in temporary things than in the Word of God. We should not be called Christians, simply because we are not following in the footsteps of our Lord.

Treating people differently

Jesus Christ of Nazareth said that His Father's house is small and that there is no room for a millionaire, but there is room for love and for friends. This does not necessarily mean that we have to be poor. Jesus Christ is telling us to love one another and not to consider some people more highly than others, for example, preferring rich people over poor people.

If we say that we love Him, then we have the honour of taking care of His church and of His children. Jesus Christ loves everybody and puts His children under His wing, He treats us well and we are a great honour to Him. Also, in the kingdom of God, we all are equal, whether rich or poor; everyone has to be treated equally.

Selfishness and wrong self-esteem

These are two major factors killing believers and slackening our spiritual development. Many of us think that we are true disciples, when there is nothing of the Gospel in us. The life of Christ and His teachings are not deeply understood, and so we cannot put the Word of God into practice.

The book of *Galatians* tells us the following:

If anyone thinks himself to be something, when he is nothing, he deceives himself. But let each one examine his own work, and then shall he have rejoicing in himself alone, and not in another. (Galatians 6:3–5)

Our selfishness and self-esteem do not help us overcome our problems, fear and misery, or enable us to enjoy the rich fruits of the Gospel.

Envy

It is amazing that many of us born-again and Spirit-filled Christians feel discontent about the good fortune of others in the body of Christ. The reason is that we are focusing on things that are physical rather than spiritual. As a result, we do not appreciate whatever we have and whatever our Maker provides for us.

We refuse to accept that we even worship the same Lord, but that our circumstances and situations are totally different. Consequently, it is not a blessing to compare ourselves to others.

Some of us also use the name of the Lord to treat people wrongly, for our own aims. The Kingdom of God is full of all these problems these days. This is simply because we do not follow in the footsteps of our Lord and do not mind doing that because of physical matters, even though we call ourselves Christians.

Jesus Christ is our only hope, in whom we stand secure. We must be well grounded in the Word of Life, stand fast and rooted in Christ, with faith to the end, so that we will not be moved by any waves.

Unfortunately, these days, we do not, and consequently we are driven by the world and experience all these problems.

Sources of Church Problems

Sources of church problems are the places from which church problems come. It is very important for us to understand this, for if there is a problem in the church, we should know how to tackle it. Church problems occur where we worship, and also apply to us ourselves.

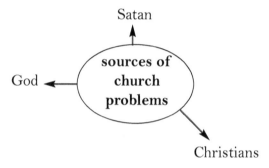

5.2: Sources of Church Problems

God

No temptation has overtaken you except such as is common to man; but God is faithful, who will not allow you to be tempted beyond what you are able, but with the temptation will also make the way of escape, that you may be able to bear it. (1 Corinthians 10:13)

According to scripture, we can see that some problems are brought about by God. Almighty God is someone whose love and care surpass all love. However, in order not to lose His people, at times He causes a problem. As Christians, we have to ask why God does that. This problem can be seen as an assessment by God of our life. He does not do this to let His people down, neither does He want to put us in a hard situation. It is so that we can know God properly in terms of His presence, power and glory, to enable us to concentrate on Him.

He knows that His light can only be manifest through the Gospel, so He makes sure that His people are aware of His existence. During this time, we sometimes feel so sad and miserable, thinking that we have nobody to help us, since we are blind to the presence of God in our life and to the spirit of God that always moves around and with us.

At times, we think that it is the work of Satan and so it may end our belief in the Lord. The outcome may be that we will have hardships, because we give up on God and allow Satan to have an opportunity to intervene in our life. In fact, it is sad that we believe that any unfair things happen to us are caused by Satan. We need an understanding that God can also cause bad things to happen to us. The Lord does these things, to let His people be serious with Him and the Gospel. Some of the bad things that God allows to happen also do us good in the long term. In many cases, we are used by God to open a better way for His people, though there may be some suffering during the problems.

Why does God cause such problems?
- to assess our faith
- to change our life
- to let us be aware of Him, His presence, love, glory and power
- to deliver us from circumstances.

Christians

I know your works, love, service, faith, and your patience; and as for your works, the last are more than the first. Nevertheless I have a few things against you, because you allow that woman Jezebel, who calls herself a prophetess, to teach and seduce My servants to commit sexual immorality and eat things sacrificed to idols. And I gave her time to repent of her sexual immorality, and she did not repent. Indeed, I will cast her into a sickbed, and those who commit adultery with her into great tribulation, unless they repent of their deeds. (Revelation 2:19–22)

This shows that we cause many of our problems, without recognising that prosperity is provided by God. It can be achieved only by doing the work of God and believing that everything comes from Him. We always rush in life and, by doing so, we are taken into a situation where we are not supposed to be.

In fact, many of the problems that we face in our life are caused by lack of understanding of the Gospel. We do not know even the basic principles of the Gospel, in order to stand by these principles in our lives. So, when there is a problem, we give up or even make the problem worse. We are totally blind to the Gospel and its fruits. It is disappointing to note that we serve God with the body, instead of serving God with the heart. We may think that the Gospel deals with physical things; however, it should be noted that it is spiritual things on which the Gospel is based. It is our responsibility to take care of physical things by using the Word of God, as well as the wisdom and knowledge that God has given to us. We should be aware that anything could allow our wisdom and knowledge to develop, and it can only be used through physical things that we encounter or see around us. This wisdom and knowledge is given to us, to protect us from unhealthy things that may happen to human kind, to enable us to have a long life.

Satan

Do not fear any of those things which you are about to suffer. Indeed, the devil is about to throw some of you into prison, that you may be tested, and you will have tribulation ten days. Be faithful until death, and I will give you the crown of life. (Revelation 2:10)

Satan is defined as the chief of evil spirits, the father of Antichrist, and the enemy of God and humans. The fall of Adam, described in Genesis 3, is the cause of all the evil, pain and suffering in creation ever since. Eating the fruit implies that Adam and Eve rejected the Word and the will of God, and loosened the relationship between God and themselves. All human beings are born with a sinful nature

148

that is inherited from our spiritual ancestor, Adam. This sinful nature acts rebelliously against God, and therefore resists the relationship with God. The sinful nature makes the body weak and controls human attitudes, behaviours and actions, and is always subject to attack by Satan to sin. Satan aims to create many problems in the body of Christ, to destroy the Gospel and to prevent us obtaining peace on this earth and everlasting lives.

Satan has some people who work for him all the time, since he is also looking for members of his kingdom, which is the kingdom of Hell. It seems that these kinds of people are true Christians, but inwardly may be the Antichrist, someone who opposes Christ and His Gospel. The father of this Antichrist is Satan, just as the father of true Christians is God. The aim of the Antichrist is to spread destruction across the world, in order to crush everyone for eternity at the second coming of Christ. How can we know that someone is the Antichrist? In fact, it is very difficult unless the Holy Spirit reveals it to us. At times, it is shown by their work and character being contrary to Christianity.

Agents are members of an organisation or society who act for it, in order for the organisation to fulfil its aims. Agents have the right to do things to help the organisation, and act in good faith to promote the organisation. Some true Christians are the agents of Satan, to gain some people for the kingdom of Satan. Satan has made willing people his agents. The information that agents bring helps the master plan to meet his aim, and, since these people are Antichrist, they always aim to destroy the work of God and God's people. Therefore, they come to the body of Christ and cause problems, to thwart the work of God or destroy our attention. Also, the master Satan can send them to cause problems.

Church Growth Elements

Church growth is the progression of Christ's church, to save the lives of God's people. This does not necessarily mean establishing churches around the world; however, it is the combination of vital factors to do the work of God sincerely, in order to have an impact on the public to come to Christ. It takes the saving of people's lives as the primary concern, and running activities to save the lives of God's people.

The elements of church growth can assist the development of the church and our ability to solve our problems and problems in the church, and to tackle Gospel proclamation tasks. We are the elements that help a church to grow.. Anything that grows depends on its source or its seed. Just as a plant grows from a seed, so does the church of God grow from its Word, which is the Bible. However, the Lord assigns the growth of the church to His followers, by giving us authority and powers to continue His work.

Therefore, all of us are physically responsible to use our gifts to accomplish this task given to us by Christ. The physical aspect here does not mean that we are exempted from spiritual things. However, what it implies is that we have to focus more on physical things than spiritual things, since it is the Lord who has authority and is totally in charge of the spiritual affairs. Truly, dealing with spiritual things is not our task; rather, we are to deal with physical things in this world. The Lord always expects us to combat the forces of this earth in His Name, and control ourselves, to give Him the glory. We have the responsibility to deal with physical things around us that will open a way for His spiritual growth and for the entire body of Christ. We must do this, rather than chasing spiritual things, which are not our responsibility. In this sense, the progression of the church of Christ to save the people's lives totally depends on us, since the task has been given to us by the Lord. We are the seed for Church growth. If we are the seed of the church growth, then we should allow God to take us, melt, mould and fill us with new life through the Holy Spirit. Then we can certainly adapt to the Gospel life system and work towards the life of Christ.

The church of God is the pillar and ground of truth for the Gospel, which represents God's instrument on earth, through which God desires to extend His Kingdom and fulfil His purpose. We are supposed to let this dream come through. However, there are some major setbacks that usually prevent us from experiencing the Gospel benefits of the work of God. Again, this influences our growth and our concentration on church development. These setbacks cause us huge problems that influence the reputation of the Gospel. In this way, if we wish to follow Christ and work toward His life, then the setbacks, caused by a lack of church growth elements, should be considered seriously. These elements are:

- better relationship reliability
- extending the relationship
- providing frequency, safety and reliability
- providing training to equip us for God's work
- creating job opportunities to help people
- advising and encouraging one another
- advancing evangelism
- better praise and worship
- genuine and deep understanding of Bible teaching.

Better relationship reliability

Like members of a family, the churches of Jesus Christ should have this reliability, since the entire body of Christ is one family. A church is a family, because the Lord Jesus Christ emphasised it thus in the Book of Life:

When Jesus Christ was preaching the Gospel, *His mother and brothers came to Him, and could not approach Him because of the crowd. And it was told Him by some, who said, "Your mother and your brothers are standing outside, desiring to see You. But He answered and said to them, "My mother and My brothers are these who hear the Word of God and do it." (Luke 8:19–21)*

A family is a group of people who are related to each other, the offspring of a mother and father. The family may consist of all the members and ancestors; it can include parents, children, relatives and servants. We are all related to the other as one body, which demonstrates love and care for others.

The church is a family because we are all doing the same work as God. It is the fellowship of the Holy Spirit that is behind the flock of the Lord Jesus Christ. The church is a family, because it has to be committed to helping and supporting each member, making the best use of their advice, assistance and the wealth of the church, as a natural family. A church is a natural family, because people are born into it, like a family of God. Therefore, it should take the responsibilities for all the members and ancestors of the church as a natural family. It is the family that a person is born into; thus, those who make up the church are supposed to raise the children and the new members, and help them, as well as the older members who may need assistance, as from a family.

The church of Jesus Christ is said to be this family, because Jesus made it clear in the book of Luke that His mother and His brothers are those who hear the Word of God and do it. A family is made up of many members and ancestors, including mothers, brothers and sisters who are under one head. Truly, one of the main aspects of a family is that we act as one body. So this statement of Jesus implies that if we have accepted Him, Jesus Christ as our personal Saviour through baptism, and do the work of the Lord, we are in His family.

All of us, no matter what nationality, origin or gender, so far as we are Christians, are in one family and act as one body. Therefore, the church has to love, support and protect all the people as a family. It has to offer support and personal development for everyone as well. The church as a family has to provide a link between all the members of the family, and be committed to assisting its members to make use of its advice and wealth, in order to have a successful in life in the future. Every effort has to be made by the members, especially the elders or the top rank, to ensure that the family members are safe and familiar with the practical aspects of life. This is as well as other necessary information we need in our everyday life, to keep us from the distractions of the modern world, since these distractions can have a serious and negative effect on our concentration on the Gospel and our lives.

Churches across the world will benefit from loving relationships, with most unbelievers coming to know God (our Father who created us) through these churches. It is a great problem these days that churches cannot unite. There is lack of unity within the entire body of Christ, and still we call ourselves disciples of Christ. If we, who are called the church of Christ, cannot unite to make one body, how can we experience the Gospel blessings? In what manner can we let the Gospel have an impact on the public?

This lack of relationship within churches affects our morale and the entire body of Christ, to the extent
that the only solution is criticism.

Extending the relationship

An *extending of the relationship* within the churches of God is one of the ways to help the Gospel reach its destination. To do this requires love, support, respect for each other and determination. We separate from each other every day, because of lack of love and respect, even though we are in the same body pursuing the same goal. This lack of love and respect, when we cannot connect to each other and solve our problems, makes it difficult for us to move forward and put our message across to the world. Maybe the dedication is there to achieve something through the blood of Christ. This means that it is a very good idea, yet things are continually getting tougher. This indicates that, in spite of all our efforts to fulfil our task of spreading the Gospel to save the lives of people, we firstly have to link to one another. Connecting to each other takes only love and respect. However, this love and respect, which will connect us to move forward, is missing.

The church is one of the key ingredients in boosting Christianity, so that the public can know Christ. It is essential for the body of Christ to embrace criticism, because of the many merits that can be obtained from this and be used effectively to help church development. There are some areas in the church, such as leadership, administration, and evangelism, that are crying out to be put right and modified, and for standards to be raised.

Providing frequency, safety and reliability

The frequency of church activities, such as worship, is necessary; however, we should understand that the safety and reliability of Christ's doctrine is of paramount importance. Many of us are using the church for different purposes to obtain our own aims. We use it to destroy people's religious beliefs, rather than to teach religion, because we do not recognise that the value of people's lives is more important than our personal worldly desires. Also, we do not realise that in no circumstances can we put a value on the loss of people's lives, the pain and distress of those who will be influenced through misuse of the church. It is very hard to understand that many do not know that the church of Christ is one of the main Gospel instruments, through which our lives will be saved. The church is a house for prayer and worship, acting as an instrument for Gospel propagation, to save the lives of God's children. We are misusing it, and using it for other things, rather than for prayer and worship, without noticing the impact on Christ's doctrine in terms of safety and reliability. It is no longer a house for prayer and worship, a place for us to spend our time, especially for those of us who are seriously determined to seek God.

Providing training to equip us for God's work

For us to use our Gospel knowledge and skills to reach people outside, we first have to be trained. This training equips us to become more efficient and effective. It also stimulates us to be part of God's work and to promote it to meet people's needs for the Gospel. Our involvement in Gospel training lets us pay particular attention to specific areas of life, and helps us find the right direction. It enables us to practise our faith, which usually develops us physically and spiritually. There are many important outcomes of training, such as support and encouragement in life. In fact, training lets us experience the Word of God and have assurance for the future, so that we can boldly share with others what we have experienced. As the proverb goes, 'seeing is believing'. We cannot talk about things we have not seen; people who share something definitely know what they are talking about.

Providing training in the Word of God should be our priority, since it is by doing the work of God that we are saved. After that, we can also reach out to proclaim the good news we have experienced. If we have really been trained in the Word of God, we are different in many aspects of life, like having a good character, which make us outstanding. Even though we are not perfect, our life will have an impact on the lives of people around us, and they will come to Christ. Most of us are not trained before we do the work of God, but believe that the Holy Spirit will take control, while we do whatever we wish. We go out to spread the good news with the aim of bringing people to Christ, while we even do not believe ourselves to be Christians. In this case, how can the message work that we share with unbelievers? Many problems in the body of Christ need to be solved before any development of the church can be successful and before it can influence people around the world. Because of a lack of training in the Word of God, our character or attitudes are holding back church progress. Our character or attitudes are the main way in which people are convinced about the Word, before they decide to accept Christ. The body of Christ needs attention and improvement to get rid of all our domineering attitudes, malpractice, selfishness and unwillingness to unite, if we want to succeed in growing spiritually and proclaiming the Gospel. We are fighting for position, members and finance in the churches, which lets us and the Gospel of Christ down. This is mostly because of the lack of Gospel training. So, if training in the Word of God is not provided, then the misuse of the Gospel and the hypocrisy of Christians will not be examined and put right, to reduce the brutal damage to the Gospel and people's lives.

Creating job opportunities to help people

Have we ever thought about what we could do in terms of our education, skills and talents, in order to create jobs for ourselves and others? Could we make a decision to bring a certain outcome that would be beneficial to the entire body of Christ? We could start the process of always assisting the church with our resources, such as money, so that the church can move on.

However, we even do not think of using some of the money we have accumulated in the church, to create jobs for others who are unemployed. Neither have we thought of using church money to sponsor people to get jobs, so that the people of God can make use of their natural talents in future. It is very surprising and sad that the same poor Christians, who always struggle to donate or give money to the church in order for the church to move on, are those who are unemployed.

Looking around, there is nothing to prove that Christians have created jobs or are doing anything considerable to help our members, although some of us establish schools. We need to impact the lives of people by creating jobs for them, to help them earn their daily bread. Doing this is a sign of loving and caring for others. Love for all of humanity does not mean accumulating money somewhere, and turning away from the suffering people, or using a domineering attitude to obtain resources from God's children for personal gain. Rather, it means respect for the sensitivity, dignity and needs of other people.

There is the issue of schools and universities. Many university and college students have been sponsored by some Christians or churches, but can find no jobs: they are qualified students and have obtained professional qualifications, but there are no jobs. If there are no jobs in the system, what is the point of establishing universities, colleges and churches? Jobs should be created for people, by Christians or churches that have plenty of money. It makes sense and it would a blessing to target the creation of jobs for people, rather than accumulating money for something else. Creating jobs for others in order to fight hunger, disease, poverty and all sorts of woes has a huge impact on the Gospel of Christ.

Advising and encouraging one another

Advice is someone's opinion and guidance for another. This advice lets people understand and know what should be done. *Encouragement* imparts confidence and provides hope. In fact, assistance given to somebody helps them make a right decision. Encouragement provides assistance to others, for them to see how to cope in a hard situation. This can come in many forms, maybe a grant of money or provision of training. Truly, we all need advice and encouragement in our everyday life.

This is very necessary in our daily life, and is really of our life. In fact, giving advice or encouragement can open or close a door for someone's success. Good advice or encouragement always leads to success, while wrong advice or discouragement puts people on the wrong track, and can even kill. Advice and encouragement are valuable to humanity, especially where problems arise or when decisions have to be made. Advising or encouraging needs a certain state of mind. Even though we are all reasonable and can solve problems, there are some problems that need really talented people to solve them.

Many of us have this talent for advising or encouraging. Using this talent would make a big change in our lives and a huge impact on other people. However, we are in the church of Christ without dedicating our talent to experience the blessing of God in our lives. On this earth we all have talents; they may not be the same, but they usually enable human kind to praise God. Therefore, if we are good at something and we refuse to dedicate to it deeply and sincerely, then something else will move us in a new direction, which might cause problems in our life. This would be the case if we do not understand how valuable our talent is and recognise how it could contribute to everyone's life.

Advising or encouraging are some of the talents God has given to us, to assist the development of His church. So we should take note and engage in a transformation process, which will promote advice and encouragement, as well as flexible Christian practice within the body of Christ. At the same time, it will minimise all sorts of domineering attitudes, if we want to experience continuing stronger growth around the world than before.

Advancing evangelism

Spreading the Gospel does not only mean moving from house to house or street to street, or organising crusades and giving leaflets with God's message to people. All these are part of spreading the Gospel. However, the most important of all is fulfilling the Word of God, not just saying it, as many of us do. Spreading the Gospel means putting the Word of God into practice, for others in the world to see and glorify God's name.

This does not mean just evangelising and quoting the entire Bible to let other people know that we are real Christians, while inwardly we are not. The Bible tells us that God awarded Paul a crown of righteousness because he turned away from unrighteous things and focused only on God, by putting the Word of God into practice.

Better praise and worship

Praise means giving thanks or blessings to God for His doings in the form of songs or poems. *Worship* is rendering honour and respect to God, in hymns or prayers. Individuals or groups can do these anywhere, though normally it is in church that we come together. What matters most is God's acceptance of the praise and worship. Praise and worship are healing tools of the Gospel. They actually act as a means through which God demonstrates His power and Gospel blessings. Through praise and worship, we come to know God intimately; we are reconciled with God, because praise and worship always remind us of what God has done for us and what God can do.

Truly, they contribute to the reduction of every temptation by the devil, and allow us to focus only on God.

Genuine and deep understanding of Bible teaching

Genuine and deep understanding of Bible teaching is the only thing that can have an effect on us. It is these teachings, through the Holy Spirit, that will enable us examine our past and present, and hopefully to do good things.

The need for genuine and deep understanding of Bible teaching does not mean that we are not teaching the Bible; what it implies here is that the majority of us are not teaching practically or with certainty from the Bible, allowing people to picture the message. We should be able to apply the real content of the Bible message into practical and physical aspects of life. It is not surprising that our failure to genuinely and deeply understand Bible teachings leads us to be more concerned with spiritual rather than practical aspects. The Bible message is totally practical, dealing with practical things that will allow spiritual things to be manifest. Spiritual affairs are always given to us, from the time that we become Christians. However, it is our responsibility to do what we are supposed to do, enabling us to experience spiritual things. Therefore, we do not need to look out any more for spiritual affairs, which indicates that we are totally blind about our Christianity.

This happens in the Kingdom of God, continually creating major problems for us. We need to proclaim the good news, to enable us to achieve our aim. This will be effective if our ministry is strongly supportive, providing sound service for the Lord's people, in both theoretical and practical ways. We need to welcome church growth elements and effectively deal with them.

6 Family

Introduction

This chapter provides a study of the relationship between our behaviour and the position of our family. The root of the family is God, and our Christian root is the family. Our daily life depends on God and the family, which determines our response. God and the family are vitally important, because they create the outcome of our life. The relationship between them shows our stability and growth. A good relationship helps us get rid of the root of our problems. Family is our root and without such a roothold we are useless.

This chapter considers children and families, studying behaviour when changes occur in our life or our family. In establishing the relationship between us and God through the linking of the Gospel, there must be a relationship between us and others, because that shows love, and love is the main root of the Gospel.

Family

A *family* is a group of people who are related to each other, sometimes known as a tribe. We all belong to this kind of family. Some families are large while others are small. A large family consists of all the members and ancestors. A small family consists of father, mother and their children. However, the size of our family has no effect on us or the Gospel of Christ. What matters most is our love for our family, not our rejection of them.

We are committed to helping our children make use of our advice and wealth, in order to succeed in the future. Parents always make an effort to ensure that their children are safe and familiar with the practical aspects of life. Members of the family also help their children by providing advice, support and assistance, especially if there is a problem. They are always willing to offer support and put their children in touch with appropriate friends or people who may be able to give assistance with specific problems.

The most important role of a family is to love, support and protect our children and family members, offering support and personal development as well. We provide invaluable support and understanding. Whatever may happen, children are under their parents' control, instead of the other way round.

Examples of a Family

There are two basic examples of family; one is called a small family and the other a large family. To let the readers gain insight into these two types of families, figures 6.1 and 6.2 below show family trees. These demonstrate all the ancestors and family members, and how they all relate to each other.

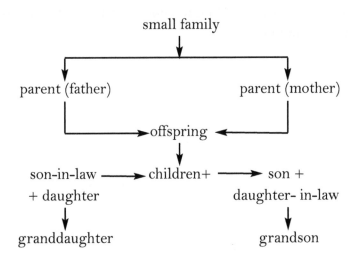

6.1: Small Family Tree

The small family comprises father, mother, children, granddaughter and grandson. However, a family commonly consists of father, mother and offspring. An example of a small family is the family of

Cain, in Genesis 4:16-25. This kind of family makes life simple and allows the family members to concentrate on their daily lives, but possibly to focus on the world's goods more than anything else. It makes people become selfish, unconcerned and not committed to other people. The people are always confined to a particular place, indicating that they are in bondage. It can be seen that there is bond of influence between the ancestors and most members of the family, for example our father and mother. When we marry, we have to concentrate on our wife and children, because they are our family. However, the bond still remains, and we are committed to also care for our parents.

The large family tree in figure 6.2 below shows another example of a family tree. This family starts from the great-grandfather and great-grandmother. An example of a large family is the family of Adam, in *Genesis 5:1-32*.If we consider all the ancestors and members of the family tree as our family, it is too large to consider as a family. However, the small or large size of the family does not matter: what counts most is the will of God, to appreciate it as a family and its benefits to human life.

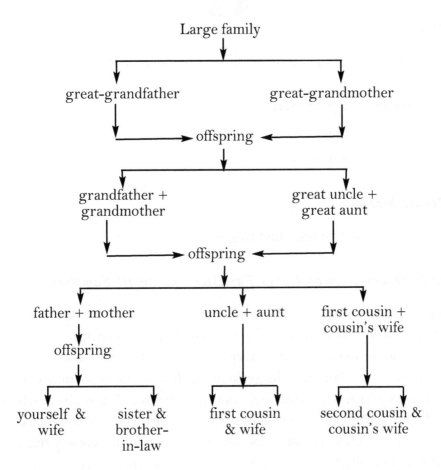

6.2: Large Family Tree

Functions of a Family

The functions of a family describe the work of parents for their children, right from the time of pregnancy. It involves hard work, and it takes love to do this kind of work, because without love, it is impossible to undertake this task of responsibility.

It seems that these days, families do not know or have forgotten their responsibilities for their children. Even if we know, we refuse to take on these responsibilities. This may be caused by the current world-situation. In fact, love is more valuable than anything else. Therefore, no matter what happens in family life, there should not be any change in our responsibilities.

Care

Every family is responsible for the care of their children.

Protection and prevention

We protect our children from danger or problems, and prevent these difficulties where possible.

Nourishment

We provide food for our child to grow, or money for the food.

Differences between Large Families and Small Families

The essence of large families is that they provide a link between all the ancestors and members of the family. This can sometimes cause problems between some members, which could have a damaging effect on all the family. In large families, all have the opportunity to develop social and practical skills in various areas of human life, such as loving, caring for others and training. There is support: assistance and valuable advice can easily be obtained from the elders at any time, which can contribute to people's success in their future lives.

Small families make it easier for people to achieve their personal ambitions; however, it does not permit the family members to show love or care for each other. If a problem arises in the family, it is likely to lead to other problems, because there is nobody to take responsibility to solve it.

Family System

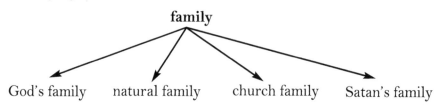

6.3: Family Systems

The family system in figure 6.3 above represents four families. Families are parental families, in which the family members are supposed to care for one another. All of us belong to at least two of these families by the end of our lives. The two families are the natural family, and God's or Satan's family.

As members of a family, we should commit totally to it, because we are part of it. It takes love, hard work and commitment to belong to a family. All family members link to each other, and this demonstrates the importance and equality of a family, no matter what we are like. We show love and concern for all in our family, and this opens a way for us to assist everyone in the family when there is need. We also believe that the affairs of family have an impact on people's lives, since the training of children starts at home before continuing elsewhere.

God's Family

Jesus answered and said to him, "Mostly assuredly, I say to you, unless one is born again, he cannot see the Kingdom of God." (John 3:3)

In his Gospel, Luke refers to the virgin conception of Jesus Christ by His mother Mary: *And the angel answered and said to her, "The Holy Spirit will come upon you, and the power of the Highest will overshadow you; therefore, also, that Holy One who is to be born will be called the Son of God." (Luke1:35)*

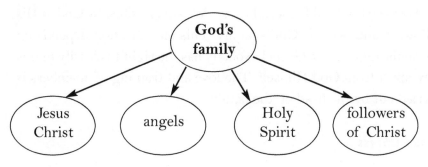

6.4: God's Family

Figure 6.4 above shows *God's family*, also known as the Creator's family (God the creator who created Heaven and earth). All the elements above work together to achieve one goal, that is, to spread the Gospel to save people's lives. God's family consists of those who do the will of God.

In the Bible, the disobedience of humans brings about separation between us and God. However, for us to acquire the nature of God, we must be born again into the family of *God (John 3: 3)*. This is a key element in becoming a member of God's family. Being born again goes further than being baptised with water. We have to be baptised with water, and with the Holy Spirit and fire. It is only by doing the will of God that we can acquire the nature of God, and be born into God's family. We assist the people of God on this earth in every way, so that they will be able to do the Gospel work. This great responsibility lies with us who have accepted Jesus Christ as our personal saviour.

Who is God? God is the Father in Heaven, who creates humans and everything around that can be seen. He is the maker and ruler of the whole world. He created Adam and Eve in the Garden of Eden. He is the father of Jesus Christ who was born of Joseph and Mary, to come and save human kind from the hands of Satan.

In this family system, He is the spiritual father of Jesus Christ, and sent Him to this earth to come and save the children of God's lives from the hands of Satan. He who created heaven and earth, the maker and ruler of the world, is the head of the family. God's family means the people who should inherit heaven. We are classified by God as His followers and become God's family. This classification depends on the application of the Gospel. Nobody has the right to classify in this way, apart from God Himself. The love and training of members is carried out by the head of the family.

Jesus Christ

Jesus Christ is a human and the Son of God, the final way to God the Father. He is the founder of the Christian religion, born of Joseph and Mary in Bethlehem, through the Holy Spirit. He is the head of all His churches. Jesus Christ came to call the people of God to be saved from Satan's hands, and to break the power of sin, so that God's people will get everlasting life. In fact, Jesus Christ's presence on this earth was to show us the divine nature of God. He was crucified on the Cross, died and was buried, and rose from death after three days. He ascended to Heaven and promised to come again in future, to judge us, the children of God, according our works.

Angels

Angels are messengers who bring God's messages to us. They could be human or superhuman.

Holy Spirit

This is the Spirit of God, who saves our lives and enables us to have future life. He acts on behalf of God and makes us act in the right way. The Holy Spirit is given to all of us, to comfort, protect and equip us for Christ's ministry.

Followers of Christ

These are people who have Christian faith, have changed from their past life, and continue to work towards Christ's life. We understand that Christianity is a journey, not a destination, so we are determined to complete the journey.

Natural Family

Then His brothers and His mother came, and standing outside they sent to Him, calling Him. And a multitude was sitting around Him; and they said to Him, "Look, Your mother and Your brothers are outside seeking You." But He answered them, saying, "Who is My mother, or My brothers?" And He looked around in a circle at those who sat about Him, and said, "Here are My mother and My brothers! For whoever does the will of God is My brother and My sister and mother."(Mark 3:31–5)

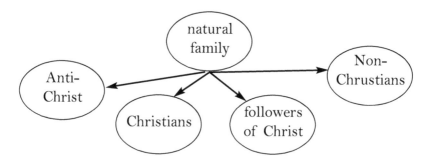

6.5: Natural Family

This *natural family* is a family that consists of a number of people in different families. It is the same kind of family that Jesus Christ was born into; Jesus had a father, a mother and brothers. When Jesus Christ was born, incense, gold and myrrh were offered to Him. This was given to Him by other people so that the parents would be able to raise Jesus Christ well.

The entire family raises any newborn baby in the family, and the parents take care of others in the family in time of need. We were all born into this kind of family. We are supposed to carry out the same responsibilities of care, protection and nourishment for our children, just as the Lord Jesus Christ's own family took care of Him, supported and protected Him.

In the family system shown above in figure 6.5, the visions of individuals in terms of religion are totally different, although we love each other as family. In this system, there may be:

- Anti-Christ, someone who denies that Jesus Christ is the Lord, and stands against the life of Christ and the teachings of the Gospel
- Christians, who believe in Christ and follow His teachings
- Non-Christians, who do not believe in Christ or follow His teachings.

Merits of family

The family lets us know our responsibilities, bring love and show care for each other. It provides fellowship for us, with care, support and personal development. It shows us our importance and parental roots. Also, it brings us together as one body, so we can learn from each other and experience human behaviour. It helps to discipline people and provides more responsibility.

Demerits of family

It creates problems, which at times lead to discrimination between the families. It also brings too much gossip that can lead to conflict.

Church Family

Do not fear any of those things which you are about to suffer. Indeed, the devil is about to throw some of you into prison, that you may be tested, and you will have tribulation ten days. Be faithful until death, and I will give you the crown of life. (Revelation 2:10)

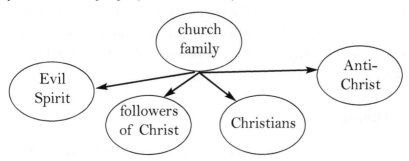

6.6: Church Family

The *church family* above refers to Christians who are the family of God the Father, the flock of the Lord, of whom Jesus Christ is the shepherd. The church is a family, because we are committed to helping all members make the best use of our advice, assistance and the wealth of the church as a natural family. The church family is almost like a natural family, because there are some members with different religious aims, such as atheists.

This church family is commonly called God's family and we are members of a church, because God is the head of the family. However, this kind of family cannot be considered as God's family.

This is simply because the quotation above shows that God's family are those people who do the will of God.

The scripture stated above is about the persecution of the church of God. This points out that not all the people in the church will enter the Kingdom of God. The devil can throw some of us into prison, since not all of us do God's will and have the same vision: some of us have a different agenda. It is hard to be in God's family because of many problems.

We are in the process of working towards the life of Christ, to enable us to become members of God's family. It is the Holy Spirit who assists this family. The Holy Spirit is in fellowship with us and guides us as the flock of Jesus Christ, to undertake our journey to a successful end.

At times, the church family is a training-ground for those who want to be members of God's family in future; family members' contributions can lead us to God's family after we die. This helps the work of Gospel, and helps us move on to achieve the Gospel vision.

In this church family system, there are: followers of Christ, Christians, Anti-Christ and the Holy Spirit.

Satan's Family

I know your works, tribulation, and poverty (but you are rich); and I know the blasphemy of those who say they are Jews and are not, but are a synagogue of Satan. (Revelation 2:9)

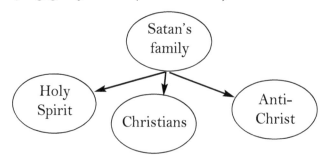

6.7: Satan's Family

Satan's family consists of the people that God has refused to welcome into His family or Kingdom. They are the people who do the will of Satan instead of doing God's will.

A synagogue is a building used by Jews for worshipping and religious instruction. However, at the time of the New Testament, this building was once described in the book of *Revelation as a synagogue of Satan (Revelation 3:9)*, which means that some people were worshipping Satan, even though they seemed to be Jews and thus God-worshippers. Some people amongst the God-worshippers were in the family of Satan, doing the work of Satan.

This links with the worship of God now, for many people in the body of Christ represent Satan like that.

This is commonly called the inheritance of Hell, of which Satan is the head. It is a type of family that cannot be seen physically, because it works spiritually. It exists on this earth and after death. This family are Antichrist and they deceive the children of God. They do not confess that Jesus Christ came in the flesh, and they deceive us in many ways, so that we do not abide in the doctrine of Christ (*2 John1: 7–8*).

This family is not like the natural and church families that we can see and express our views about, since this type of family does not aim to do us any good, but is always secretly looking for our downfall. Satan is always the head of this family; however, there are many leaders within the family.

Comparisons

God's family consists of people who are actually called followers of Christ, which means that we deeply understand that Christ has rescued us from our sins, so we are truly committed to the teachings of Christ, no matter what happens to us. We are those people who have changed from our past lives and put on new lives. We yield our lives to God, to be illuminated by the presence of the Lord. God's family depends on the application of the Bible and the teachings of the Gospel.

With the natural family, the head of the family has an effect on the family members. Natural and church families can be seen physically and experienced on the earth. In them, there are many problems and difficulties. However, what makes natural families different is that the responsibilities are taken by the family. Family members normally care for one another, despite problems that can arise. It is just like God's family because there is love.

In the church family, nobody wants to take any responsibility, since we think that whatever happens to us is God's responsibility. God may be in control of everything, but the leaders are supposed to manage this family and to undertake Gospel work with the help of the Holy Spirit. It is our responsibility, especially the leaders, to do the work of the Church family, rather than expecting God to do it, as many think.

Within the church family, the leaders are the heads of the family, and have an effect on the members of the family; the Holy Spirit acts as the guide of the family. The church family comprises many families, since some are Satan's family and natural families. Some of us are in two families at the same time; however, we have the aim of becoming part of the family of God, before we die if possible. The church family is very important because it is the main source of God's family, with people coming from it to inherit the Kingdom of God.

The main differences between God's family and the other families are that in God's family, there is love and no death, sickness or poverty. God, the creator of all things, is the head of the family and everyone is entitled to the benefits of the family.

Christian Family

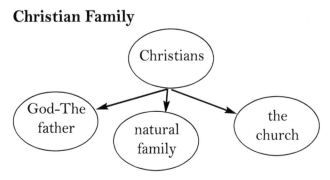

6.8: *Christian Family*

The figure (6.8) above shows three families, to enable us to realise that all of us have three main families to focus on in our life, as far as the Gospel is concerned. It is our responsibility to see that parental love and protection should not be thwarted or broken. In this sense, no one should permit circumstances or worldly goods to ruin the achievements of Christ for us and our families.

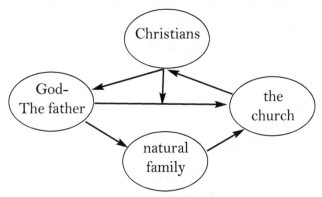

6.9: *Christian Parental System*

The *Christian parental system* in figure 6.9 above describes our families and their relationship. It shows us the nature of each family, what they mean, and how they connect to each other.

The relationship is very necessary in our life, since it shows love and fear of God, which is a key tool in Christ's Gospel and can open a way for us to succeed in life. It is shameful to realise that most of us do not consider our fellow Christians as family. We are indeed all mothers, brothers and sisters in one body, since we are all followers of Christ.

Jesus Christ's Family

Jesus Christ's Family consists of three: God's family (*John 3:3*), natural family (*Luke 2, Luke 8:19–21*) and church family (*Revelation 2:10*).

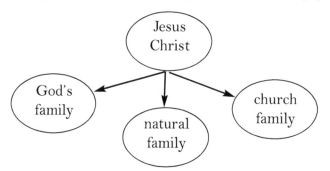

6.10: *Jesus Christ's Family*

Jesus Christ's family above represents the types of families of the Lord Jesus Christ. These families are the main ones that now represent the families of all true believers. This system is the biblical requirement for Christian families. We Christians should commit to them totally, as we are parts of the Body of Christ.

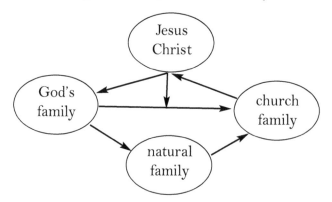

6.11: *Jesus Christ's Parental System*

Jesus Christ's parental system in figure 6.11 above shows the families of Jesus Christ and their importance to us. The components work together to achieve a goal. The goal is to spread the Gospel of Christ to save people's lives. The Lord Jesus Christ was able to fulfil this goal by overcoming Satan, by taking these three families as His main priority, though at times He was very harsh to some of the people in these families. However, it does not mean that He did not like us. An example is when Jesus Christ said, *"My mother and My brothers are these who hear the word of God and do it." (Luke 8:21)*

Jesus Christ's parental system illustrates how each part connects to another and how they work together to achieve one goal. It demonstrates the importance and equality of human beings, no matter what we are like and where we come from. The relationship is very necessary in our life, because it shows that love and care for others are key tools to Christ's Gospel and can open a way for us to succeed in life. This relationship has an effect on our life with regard to nationality, religion and personality, since the three components link and work together, to enable God to fulfil His plans for love and to allow His children to love each other to obtain future life.

Jesus Christ's Anger

Jesus Christ's anger is seen in two places in the Bible: *Mark 11:15–17* and *Luke 8:19–21*. There are two themes: lack of mercy, and rejection.

Lack of mercy

The *lack of mercy* of the Lord is shown towards those who were trading in the Temple:

Jesus went into the temple and began to drive out those who bought and sold in the temple, and overturned the tables of the moneychangers and the seats of those who sold doves. And He would not allow anyone to carry wares through the temple. Then He taught, saying to them, "Is it not written, 'My house shall be called a house of prayer for all nations'? But you have made it a 'den of thieves.'"(Mark 11:15–17)

Rejection

His mother and brothers came to Him, and could not approach Him because of the crowd. And it was told Him by some, who said, "Your mother and your brothers are standing outside, desiring to see You". But He answered and said to them, "My mother and My brothers are these who hear the Word of God and do it." (Luke 8:19–21)

Characteristics of Jesus Christ's Anger

Anger is the emotion of feeling hurt by someone or about something. This anger is our expression of emotion about something that has happened, which can cause many problems. There are many sources of anger; however, people's attitudes and sin are the main two sources.

Jesus Christ's speech about his family when they called Him, may be considered here as anger; at that time, He felt displeasure at what His mother Mary and His brothers did and He hit out at them. This anger needs to be understood, so that we may deeply understand the teachings and the importance of Christ's Gospel.

The main characteristic of His anger was that it surely did not break His relationship with His mother and brothers. So it was not wrongful disobedience, neither was it rejection, but the expression of Gospel necessities and care. He was angry to show the importance of the Gospel and to open a way for the advancement of His Kingdom across the world. Therefore, it may not always be wrong to be angry if it will help to put things right, enabling something good in the future.

Characteristics of Jesus Christ's and Human Anger

The main differences between Jesus Christ's anger and human anger is that Jesus Christ's anger is the expression of concern and care. It was not hateful, breaking relationships or friendships, though it was seen as a sin against His people. However, Jesus knew that this 'sin' would do His children good.

The same applies to human life. At times, we see our children doing the wrong thing one way or another that will not help them in the long run. Doing this does not mean that we do not love our children.

Truly, we love them as Jesus did, because He loved us so much that He could not afford to lose us. He did that to save our lives, therefore whatever we do, we need to consider its outcome, as the Lord did. He did an excellent job by cleansing the Temple, rather than doing evil to the people.

Human anger, however, is a feeling that at any time we might break or destroy something. Human anger is hateful, and is hard to control, unless it destroys something or someone.

Causes of Anger

The causes of anger are things that make us feel strong displeasure and turn against others. Any anger has a cause and the action of anger may be hitting, speaking or damaging. These are some of the main causes:

- Disappointment - someone fails to fulfil our wish
- Unfaithfulness – someone does not perform their duties or does not keep their promise
- Attitude - someone misbehaves towards us
- Situation - some circumstances or conditions affect people; for example, they feel lonely or have no money to cater for their needs
- Failure - someone is unable to do something for us
- Theft – someone steals something of ours
- Dispute - someone argues with us about something
- Noise – someone causes too much noise.

Outcome and control of anger

The *outcome of anger* can be good or bad, though in most cases, the outcome of anger is bad. Anger always has two effects – one on us and the other on the person who causes it. When we are angry, it can lead us to destruction, which can affect our everyday life. The one who causes anger can be in a situation of fear and sadness that might contribute to the failure of their life in many areas. Anger can break relationships and destroy individuals. So, whether good or bad things might come of it, we should not allow it to happen.

Two typical examples of anger that led to destruction can be seen in the Bible. One is where the Lord Jesus Christ was angry in the Temple, and people's goods were destroyed, which was a very bad thing to do to His children; however, saving His children's lives was its result. The second example of sinful anger and a bad outcome was when the people provoked Moses, as narrated in the Old Testament. *The Israelites complained to Moses and his brother about the wilderness, provoking their anger: Moses and Aaron gathered the assembly together before the rock; and he said to them, "Hear now, you rebels! Must we bring water for you out of this rock?" (Numbers 20:10)*

Control of anger means the tools that can be used to regulate or prevent our anger. There are three key tools: the Word of God, since it does us good to always pray to God to help us get rid of it. The second tool is to try to laugh in time of anger. The other tool is to speak slowly when we are getting angry. It is even better to try not to speak at all, rather than speak in anger. These tools control our anger that might otherwise cause problems for us and for others.

Importance of Jesus Christ's Speech of Rejection

This statement by the Lord Jesus Christ confirms the strength of His anger at the time. It also implies that He did reject His family at a certain time. However, the love that He showed to His mother proves that, inwardly, He did not reject His mother and His brothers, who were part of His family. The speech was to let the people of God then and now understand and value the Gospel more than anything else in our lives. In fact, the Lord told people that the Gospel is our future life. So, we have to make it our first priority and focus on it all the time. Rather than walking out on His family, what He was doing at that moment was more vital than anything else, and He wanted the people to notice that.

Effects of Family Rejection

His mother and brothers came to Him, and could not approach Him because of the crowd. And it was told Him by some, who said, "Your mother and your brothers are standing outside, desiring to see You". But He answered and said to them, "My mother and My brothers are these who hear the Word of God and do it."(Luke 8:19–21)

What does Christ's speech mean to us? Why did Christ reject His family at that moment, and what is its importance? What does family rejection mean?

It means that a family has been refused for some reason. Here, it applies to us when we refuse our family, friend or others since we became Christians. This is booming now, as if it is a biblical requirement.

It may be that family or people are unworthy, harmful or do not love us. However, the question is whether it is right, as disciples of Christ, to reject such people. Did Jesus Christ reject His family? If so, did He bring peace of mind to His parents and the world at large? We throw our family away as if they are useless for several reasons. The families have become a great enemy to us, and we treat them in a way that is generally contrary to the Gospel.

However, in the whole of the Gospel, Jesus Christ did not reject His family; on the cross, He told a disciple to take His mother Mary home and comfort her. Asking this of the disciple means that He did love His family and cared for them. Jesus Christ spoke these influential words while He was on the cross:

When Jesus therefore saw His mother, and the disciple whom He loved standing by, He said to His mother, "Woman, behold your son!" Then He said to the disciple, "Behold your mother!" (John 19:26–7)

Jesus' statements towards His mother show us the importance of a family and how we have to love our parents and to provide for them as well. In so doing, we show our love for Jesus and God our Maker.

Do we born-again Christians now love our families as Jesus Christ did? Definitely not. Most of us even think that, because we have become Christians, we have to reject our families or walk out on them, since our families:

- are not Christians or are unbelievers
- go to a different Church of God
- are devils, we think
- oppose our marriage

Unbelievers have not accepted Jesus Christ as their personal Saviour through baptism and do not follow His teachings. Though these people may or may not have faith in God, they have no duty and responsibility to believe God and His Word, learn, study it and put it into practice. They may hear about the Gospel of Christ, read the Bible and Christian books, do charity work, love and care for other people. However, they are not Christians. They are free people, since they do whatever they like. However, they cannot stand up to problems such as poverty, sickness and distress, since they do not believe and rely on the Word of God for a breakthrough, knowing that God is keeping them safe. So they give up easily and at times some take their own life.

Firstly, is it right for us to reject these people in our families? If it is right that we reject or walk out on them because they are unbelievers, then why do we want people in the world to come to God's Kingdom? Are our parents not in the same world? What is the purpose of the coming of Jesus Christ, and of evangelism? Did Jesus Christ of Nazareth come because of the righteous people or the sinners? The Maker of all things Himself did not reject us. He loves us and welcomes us to His Kingdom, so who are we to reject or walk out on our families because they are unbelievers? If we have rejected our families because they are not Christians, why do we go outside to evangelise in order to bring someone else's family who are also not Christians to the Kingdom of God? Will this work? Where in the Book of Life does it tell us to reject unbelievers? How can we experience the power of our God by rejecting or walking out on our families because they are unbelievers? Did God come because of righteous people like us? We need to think about it very carefully and assess ourselves in this situation.

Secondly, do we have to reject our families for going to different churches of Christ? Let us ask ourselves if Jesus Christ is the head of all the Christian churches, and if the same Bible is used by these churches. In fact, as human lives constantly increase in number, the churches of God also increase; because of this, there are many churches of God around the world. These churches preach the same doctrine of Jesus Christ and use the same Bible. The Christian books some of us use may be different, depending on the writers. However, the important thing is that all Christian books are about the doctrine of Jesus Christ. So, if our family goes to these one of these other churches where the same Gospel of Christ is preached, is this wrong? Even if they do not, is it right to reject them?

It is amazing that many believers have become enemies since they go to different churches. Some parents, families or friends feel unwanted or unworthy, because they go to other churches, and they also suffer from rejection. Do our church differences matter more than the God we worship?

Thirdly, if we think that our families are devils; do we have to reject them? What is a devil? It is an evil spirit, and is sometimes also known as Satan. Some human beings possess this evil spirit. Clearly, anyone who possesses this kind of evil spirit is an evil person, and is not interested in good things. Thus, such people are total enemies of goodness, and have the power to do whatever they want on this earth, against the Word of God. They can kill, destroy, harm, and be a bad influence. They commit all sorts of malpractice to destroy humankind.

As Christians, do we have to reject such people? Entirely not, even though some Christians normally do. Surely, any of us who reject such people do not know the kind of God we worship. Certainly, we have to take care of our family, especially those who are unbelievers and even beyond, since doing this will make us different among them, and will let the others know the kind of God we worship. This will influence them to come to Christ, for the Lord to demonstrate His love and power to get rid of the evil spirit they possess. Therefore, we do not need to reject such people.

Why should we reject them, even if they possess evil spirits or are Satan's agents? Do we not know our position with the Lord? *Luke 12:4* tells us not to fear anyone who kills the body, but rather to fear Him who kills the body and afterwards has the power to cast us into hell. Moreover, if we fear devils, then we are saying that Jesus Christ of Nazareth did not overcome devils on the cross, and that the God we worship is powerless to have authority over devils. As a result, we ourselves have no power over devils. Also, we have allowed Satan to defeat us, and automatically we will never experience the work of Holy Spirit in our life.

Fourthly, must we reject our family if they oppose our wedding? Opposing means resisting someone or something. Opposition has become part of human life. A family may be against our idea of getting married. The may be because we are not mature enough, or do not have the money for the wedding expenses. We may believe that this is the most opportune time for us to get married, no matter the circumstances. As a result, they become enemies and are rejected by us.

Is it right for us to reject our family for opposing a wedding? If we reject our family, how can we possibly ask for God's blessings? Are we Christians who make bad times sweet and bad things good, as our God wants us to? Do we regard ourselves as dear and kind Christians whose whole lives are a witness for Jesus Christ? This rejection has a damaging impact on the Gospel at large. It also affects three major areas: Christians, family and the public

Effects on the Gospel

It goes against the Ten Commandments, influences the Gospel reputation and the proclamation of the Gospel.

Effects on Christians

If we reject our family, who suffers most, us or the family? Truly, we suffer the most in the long run. It affects our life, both physical and spiritual, and makes our Christianity useless. Also, it reduces our spiritual growth, brings separation between God and us, and reduces our concentration on the Gospel.

Effects on family

It discourages them from coming to Christ if they are unbelievers, and reduces the love and respect they have for us. It breaks the relationship between both parties.

Effects on the public

It discourages the public from respecting disciples of Christ, and unbelievers from coming to Christ.

This rejection means that we are not salt and light in our family. The Book of Life says that Christians are the salt and light in their family and in the world. So, what are we? The rejection of our family means that we do not know our position in Christ and what Christianity is all about, and, as a result, we abuse it. If our families are unbelievers, go to different churches or we think that they are devils, as Christians, it is our responsibility to pray for them and let the Holy Spirit do the rest, but not reject them or walk out on them. If the Word of Life says that we are salt and light, then we are supposed to be in the darkness and shine in that darkness. Therefore, if we reject or walk out on our family, what is the purpose of being Christians?

Being Christians means going to church and worshipping the Lord, quoting all the verses from Genesis to Revelation, speaking in tongues, obeying and respecting a few Christians that we know. Doing this does not mean that we are Christians, even though they are part of it. This rejection of our family means that we are not putting the Word of Life into practice, which is the most important aspect of being born-again Christians. If we reject our family, what position do we have in Christ?

Jesus Christ of Nazareth did not come because of righteousness and material things. He came because of sinners and to demonstrate to us practically and not theoretically. All that Jesus Christ did was practical. He came to show us the things we should and should not do, for us to know the right way to follow His steps, to enable us to have authority and power to dominate this world, in order to give Him all the glory.

Are we Christians following in Jesus our Maker's footsteps? What is amazing is that we are even more spiritual than our Maker, to the point that the Holy Spirit, who is our helper and comforter, fears to come near us. Thus the house of the Lord is full of woes and works of Satan.

May the Lord have mercy on us and get rid of all baby-Christian thinking and behaviour. This will help us grow spiritually, to see and do wonders as our Lord Jesus Christ did.

7 Love your Enemies

Introduction

This chapter is about the problems that can be expected between neighbours, the solution to such problems, and the opportunities that have to be realised for us to apply love in our lives.

An important requirement for human beings is that there should be love. For us to be successful in life, there should be assistance, and this does not come from nowhere. It is not our efforts that make us successful. Our efforts do contribute greatly, but in most cases it is help from others. This help cannot happen without love, because love is valuable and creates a special relationship between people, with good results. Any loving relationship lasts longer, even if some problems occur. This love brings people together. With love, our responsibilities change and charge us to take care of each other.
This chapter demonstrates the importance of loving one another, and considers practical ways of dealing with problems.

I say to you, love your enemies, bless those who curse you, do good to those who hate you, and pray for those who spitefully use you and persecute you, that you may be sons of your Father in heaven; for He makes His sun rise on the evil and on the good, and sends rain on the just and on the unjust. (Matthew 5:44–5)

Enemies

An *enemy* is a person or group that hates and tries to harm another. Enemies always oppose one another and may even wish to harm each other. We do not like each other, and do not want to see each other, because it does not make us feel good. Enemies can also be when two countries are at war, when brother and sister hate each other and when one animal devours another.

Enemies are people who:
- hate us
- curse us
- wish to hurt or make us suffer
- persecute us – people who treat us badly or trouble us by repeated attacks.

Love your Enemies

Loving your enemies means showing a strong feeling for the people who dislike, curse, hurt or persecute us. It is the recognition of our need for Christ's blood, to forgive those people who we think are our enemies through all sorts of hatred, and to love them. Figure 7.1 above depicts Jesus Christ and the Samaritan woman, which is an example of loving an enemy. Jesus Christ loved a Samaritan woman, who was His enemy, by approaching her and having a chat.

7.1: Jesus Christ and the Samaritan woman

Loving our enemies means continuing support and fellowship, to maintain and develop a concrete relationship between partners. It shows our care for people and lets us know God. As Christians, it enables us to live out our faith and blessings in time of problems. It lets the power of God be manifest in our everyday life, and influences our enemies' lives as well, to show them the importance of the Gospel to humankind.

Jesus Christ tells us to love these enemies, as He loves us. We should bless those who persecute us, do these people good and pray for them. Loving these people is not verbal love, but is expressed as brotherly love. The Bible tells us that if these people are hungry and thirsty, we should feed them and give them drink. It continues to say that we have to behave like Christians, not be overcome by evil, but overcome evil with good. We can only achieve this by not repaying anyone evil for evil. Furthermore, it says that if we do not love these people, then we are not clinging to what is good, and as a result, we are denying Him since we do not love Him.

However, some difficult questions arise here: how can we love, do good and pray for our enemies who hate us and even wish to kill or destroy us? Why does our Lord ask us to love such people? It seems impossible. It is not easy, yet Jesus Christ the Lord Himself showed us an example of loving our enemies. He did this by asking a Samaritan woman, who had come to get some water from a well, to give Him a drink. At that time, there were problems between Jews and Samaritans; their two countries hated each other. Jesus Christ was a Jew, so they were enemies facing problems, as most of us do. Despite this hatred, the King of kings asked His enemy, the Samaritan woman, for a drink of water.

Why did He do this, when He knew that they did not get on? Can we really love our enemies and even talk to them physically, as the Lord did? This is not mental love, but *agape* love, which deals with heart- commitment. Even if it is a mental love, we as His disciples cannot do what our Lord did. There are some implications that may help us to reconcile with our enemies and love them, to do good to them and pray for them.

Why did the woman respond to Jesus her enemy, since she also knew that Jesus Christ was a Jew? It surprised the woman so much that she asked why He requested a drink of water.

These are some of the important issues that we will examine and bring to our lives, with their moral, social, cultural and personal issues, to help us achieve our aims of being followers of Jesus Christ. First of all, the Master knew that His ambitions for coming to this world had nothing to do with things of this world. Secondly, He was aware that loving His enemy would open ways for Him to achieve His objectives. Thirdly, He knew that the Samaritan woman was His enemy, yet she needed help and salvation. He did not ignore the woman when He saw that she was in hardship and that she needed His assistance, despite all the conflict between the two countries.

Jesus knew that their differences did not matter; what mattered most was their human nature. Through this, He demonstrated love to prove His concern about her life. However, this major loving step from the Lord made the woman flexible, and brought conversation between them. As a result, the woman talked to her Maker, and was surprised to receive blessings. Moreover, Jesus Christ was able to proclaim His message, and gave people everlasting life to fulfil His ambition.

Factors in Loving our Enemies

Loving our enemies is a hard task, but there are some factors that can help us do it:
- prayer
- ambition
- destiny
- heart-commitment

Prayer is seeking God and making supplication, and the intercourse of the soul with God. It is drawing near to God and pouring out our soul before the Lord. There are many kinds of prayer such as social, secret and public prayer. Social prayer is a prayer that deals with a family, and secret prayer is about a personal issue. Public prayer is about praying for a country or the world at large.

Ambition is a desire to work hard to achieve a goal. It is doing our best at everything in order to be successful. For example, someone's ambition and desire was to become a pastor and the person has really worked hard to achieved it

Destiny is when something happens which is meant to be. This implies that, as human beings, there is something for each one of us to become which will make us human. Destiny, on other hand, is spiritual in nature and deals with the practising of spiritual matters in order to overcome them. Our destinies are not the same: each one of us has a different destiny.

Heart-commitment is determining to do something, even when things get tougher. It is regular action and dedication, to accomplish a task or goal. Heart-commitment is based on action, willingness and sacrifice to complete something successfully, even though there will be difficulties on the way.

Kindness

Then the woman of Samaria said to Him, "How is it that You, being a Jew, ask a drink from me, a Samaritan woman?" For Jews have no dealings with Samaritans. (John 4:9–10)

The Lord Jesus Christ tried to help the Samaritan woman and make her happy.

As Christians, what do we do if someone does us wrong? Do we avenge ourselves or not? Do we look and behave like true Christians?

Now it is we ourselves who create problems and confusion, even in the same church. Christ's churches have become enemies to each other; families have become enemies to their children who are Christians. We believers undermine the Gospel by turning away from the main channels of the Gospel. We do not trust ourselves, and neither does the public trust us, since our behaviour is not in keeping with our teaching. The Lord knows that if we refuse to love our enemies, then we are undermining the Gospel. Also, fighting against our enemies is nothing and repaying someone evil for evil is nothing, but keeping the Word of God is what matters. We have to do the same thing as Jesus Christ did, by examining ourselves carefully and putting His examples into practice.

Truly, loving our enemies is a very hard thing to do, yet it has so many benefits. It will help and open us to receiving our blessings, to glorify our Lord and through that will enable us to achieve our aims.

Merits of Loving our Enemies

It manifests the power of God, proclaims that God is King of kings and shows who the true Christians are. It closes a wooden door and opens golden doors. It brings salvation and peace, brings us back from sin, and reconciles us with others. It enables us to learn and know the truth, achieve our objectives. It proclaims the Gospel.

With all the advantages of loving our enemies, the two enemies also gain from it, because a relationship is restored. Loving our enemies is always a great benefit to humanity.

Benefits to Jesus Christ of loving His enemy

It opened ways for Jesus Christ to put His message across to the people, to achieve His ambition and fulfil His Ministry.

And many of the Samaritans of that city believed in Him because of the woman who testified, "He told me all that I ever did." (John 4:39)

Christ was able to save people's lives wherever He went.

Then they said to the woman, "Now we believe, not because of what you said, for we ourselves have heard Him and we know that this is indeed the Christ, the Saviour of the world." (John 4:42)

Benefits to the Samaritan woman

Once the Samaritan woman recognised Jesus Christ as the true Messiah, she confessed her sins and repented, and she was forgiven and received salvation. The woman received her blessings and Jesus Christ solved her problems.

Benefits to the public

After this incident, many Samaritans believed in Jesus Christ as their Saviour, repented and became believers. People were saved and their problems were solved. (*John 4: 39–41*)

Ways of Functioning

Ways of functioning is the manner in which enemies work. One of these commonest is a curse, when we ask God or Satan to bring harm or evil upon someone. We want someone to suffer some hardship or loss because of their bad character. This curse may occur because of hatred and anger about someone's wrongdoings. Every curse is operated by evil and does not just happen. Truly, any curse has an effect on a person, and sooner or later it will happen. However, not all curses work, because before a curse can work, it needs something to support it. A curse usually destroys the life of a person, and at times it can kill them.

There are three basic forms of curses: *self-inflicted, ancestor-inflicted, and neighbour-inflicted* curses.

Self-inflicted curses are curses we ourselves cause, such as swearing, unnecessarily, that we do not drink and cheat, while we do all these things. By saying these things, we are asking God to bring harm upon us, and we can suffer from the words. One thing we should bear in mind is that this curse is not operated by the Devil: it is operated by God, since we believe that God can forgive this kind of curse. If we realise that we have sinned, we can confess, repent and apply the blood of Jesus Christ to forgive our sin, since God is not like the Devil or us when we condone human sinful life.

An example of a self-inflicted curse can be seen in *Genesis 3:17: Then to Adam He said, "Because you have heeded the voice of your wife, and have eaten from the tree of which I commanded you, saying, 'You shall not eat of it': Cursed is the ground for your sake: in toil you shall eat of it all the days of your life."* Adam caused harm to himself, which is a punishment from God; he brought this upon himself.

An *ancestor-inflicted* curse is the suffering or harming of the great-grandfathers, which has now become an ancestral trait in the family. The suffering or harming from a curse will be possible only if the curse has a root to support it. So, in the case of an ancestor-inflicted curse, there is a root. Since the curse is inherited and has a cause, it is likely that the people in the family will be influenced by the curse.

They will suffer from it, though they may not know about it; in fact, this kind of curse may land on us. It can surely be broken and set free by the Word of God, because we in the family who suffer later are not the ones who did the wrong thing. So, there are consequences of the curse.

A *neighbour-inflicted* curse does not only mean that someone who lives nearby can ask God or Satan to bring evil upon us. What is implied here is that any human being can curse us to suffer in life, as long as we have done wrong to them. There are many ways of doing wrong to others, so that they can curse us and cause us suffering. Some of these ways are: cheating, stealing or bad temper that insults us unnecessarily. In fact, doing these can cause us many problems, because the curse will function. We often do make mistakes by thinking that, because we are born again, we can do whatever we wish to our neighbours and we can get away with it. That is totally childish, because if we are Christians, it does not mean that we can step on someone's toe and go free. Even Christianity is based on principles and the Word of God works in accordance with these principles. Therefore, if we do not stay within the principles, then we are responsible for dealing with the matter ourselves. In fact, we must not be mistaken and think that God will not comfort us, guard and protect us; the Lord will definitely do that as He always does. However, we will receive the outcome of what we have done. So, we should be very careful because we are born again: curses can influence us. We should be aware that curses have roots, and will therefore affect us.

Victimising

A *victim* is anyone who suffers some hardship or loss because of other people's bad character, and who might have suffered insult, theft or cheating. So, *victimising* is concerned with doing wrong things to other people, thus breaking the law. Victims sometimes get upset by people's attitude or character to such an extent that they curse them. If offenders do something wrong even though they intend to ask their victim to forgive them, then the victims cannot get away with the curse.

It is so tiring when we moan about people who we consider as our enemies and curse them. In fact, if we wish to grow up in Christianity, we should not expect others to do God's work for us. If we do moan about enemies all the time, then we are letting others take our authority and power, which we should use to stand against other forces. Moaning about our enemies is not consistent with our growth, both in our physical and spiritual life, and will not gain us comfort and peace. We have to think about the work of God, which is the weapon to fight enemies. If we choose to focus on the work of God, we are supposed to use the work of God to protect and defend ourselves from anything that will put our lives at risk. Why are we more concerned about our enemies than about doing the work of God? If curses are uttered by enemies or witches against others, and have no cause, they will never influence anyone; we who are cursed will be free of them.

Examples of victimising

These are some examples:

Cheating: we are wrongly treated or taken advantage of and deceived.

Stealing: our belongings are stolen.

Bad temper: we are insulted by someone's bad temper.

Blasphemy: others might speak evil and lies, about us or against God or Christianity. They might give deeply felt offence, or utter abuse or calumny against us, which will cause harm, stumbling or downfall, simply through the thoughtless exercise of their freedom. (*Romans 14:15-16*)

Solving Curses and Curse Control

Solving curses is when we have been cursed, we can deal with it in order to be set free. There are two main ways of dealing with curses:

God, and us. If we have been cursed, we can ask God to forgive the wrongdoing. If we are the cursers, we can contact those we have cursed and ask for forgiveness. Solving these curses actually depends on us.

Self-inflicted curses

It is God only who can forgive such curses. The Lord will forgive the harm or suffering that comes to people, if we heartily confess our wrongdoings or saying bad words, and truly stop doing them.

Ancestor-inflicted curses

God and the family can solve this curse. If we as family members understand the root of the curse and know the victim, we can contact the victim personally and solve the problem. However, if we do not know the victim, then we can seek God's forgiveness. The Word of God will solve the curse, when we believe we have done nothing wrong to let the curse happen. On the other hand, the Word of God can break the curse and uproot any problems caused by the curse in the family, through our responsibility as family members.

Neighbour-inflicted curses

There are two options. First, God can be asked to forgive the harm or suffering that has been called on others. Secondly, we can contact the victims and ask them to forgive us. The best way to solve the problem is for us to go to the victims personally and ask for forgiveness. The Word of God can break the curse and set free the offenders or victims. However, restoring the relationship between two people is vitally important; in fact, it is necessary, because it will help both of them to continue and concentrate on their daily lives. Certainly, it will wipe away the victim's hardship or loss and give them peace of mind. The offenders will be relieved from curse problems. They will understand the consequences of offending other people, which will prevent them from doing more wrong. It will transform them and let them focus on the Word of God more than anything else. So it is better for the offenders to seek the victims personally and ask forgiveness; having done that, the offenders can seek God's forgiveness.

Curse control means what should be done to prevent curses. Curses can be controlled by repentance and telling the truth about what we have done. In fact, the most suitable way to control curses is by doing God's work through the Holy Spirit. If we do the work of God, it is likely that we cannot easily be cursed, since we will be submitted to God, and so the Holy Spirit may protect us. As the Holy Spirit becomes dominant in our daily life, we will be free from the law of sin. At the same time, the Holy Spirit will usher in a holy and fruitful life.

In *John 7:38*, Jesus Christ spoke of the work of the Holy Spirit as *rivers of living water*. This implies that our life will be constantly flowing in and out of the Holy Spirit. However, if we continue to submit to the Holy Spirit by doing God's will, we can relate to the Holy Spirit as a person. This will enable us to control curses and experience the peace of God in our life through the Holy Spirit.

Good Samaritan

A *Samaritan* is a person who helps others in trouble, distress and difficult situations, to save their lives. We give or provide others with something needed to help them improve their lives and cope with their everyday problems. People can die without assistance in trouble, distress or want. In some ways, it is necessary to stop our busyness and consider others' lives, if they need us to relieve their trouble and save their lives. Samaritans are not selfish in helping others.

Example of a Good Samaritan

Luke 10:30-37 tells the story of the Good Samaritan, a traveller who helped another traveller who had been beaten and robbed by thieves.

Are we Good Samaritans these days, and do we help one another? The Bible says that Jesus Christ, the Master Himself, cared for others. He had time for His fellow humans. He forgot his busyness, and had time to heal the sick, teach people and explain the message in the Bible, share and solve problems, forgive sins, and advise people.

Jesus Christ demonstrated his love and care for the world by doing many things. Truly, our Lord concentrated on people's success, as well as creating situations for them. These days, we do not want to see or know our brothers' and sisters' problems, or even have a few minutes for them when they are in crisis. We always have the excuse of our personal achievements.

Is it right for us to be called born-again Christians? It is hard to believe that we desire to be called Christians, because our motives for worshipping God are totally contrary to the Lord. Jesus Christ came to save and care for all of us, by carrying the cross. God was not selfish and selective. He did not say that He was a Jew here for Jews only. Neither did He come to save only His family, but the whole world. He took the consequences of our sin and saved all of us. So, as His disciples, we are supposed to do the same thing, if we boldly declare that we are His true disciples.

These days, we are always very busy with activities that will bring us money or our personal achievements, rather than sharing, helping or solving others' problems. Does the Book of Life tell us to forget others and focus on our own needs? Are our activities more important than others, who need our presence or help at a particular time? At times, our activities may be more important than other matters. Yet the Bible does not tell us to consider our own matters first, but rather to consider who is in need at a particular moment.

The Bible makes it clear that the Good Samaritan was very busy travelling, but as soon as he came across a sick person on his way, who was desperately in need of help, this Samaritan was kind and loving, and gave his best assistance to the sick man. But a Priest and then a Levite passed by this sick man because of the work they were going to do. It was made clear in the Bible that these religious men were not true followers of God, but the Samaritan was declared a lover of God. These days, the Priest and the Levite might be pastor, prophet or born-again Christian.

Why was the Samaritan classified as a true worshipper instead of as an unbeliever? What could happen with the people who passed by? Did they not go to worship God every week? Were they not very busy going somewhere, perhaps to preach? This shows us that Jesus is not looking for status or position, but rather for kindness and the love that we have for others. Through the kindness and love from the Samaritan, the King of kings classified him as His follower and welcomed him in to His kingdom. We must be aware that our Lord is more interested in our care for others.

What is our position? Can we classify ourselves as followers of Jesus Christ, as the Samaritan was? Most of us these days are always busy, for ourselves or the few people we relate to. Some of us even pretend to be busy, in order to get away from helping others in need or sharing others' problems or difficulties. The difficult question that arises here is whether we understand the message of Christ. Probably we do understand it, but instead, we pursue the things of the world. The Bible states that such people are certainly not called Christians, though we declare ourselves true believers in Christ.

Jesus declared to His disciples, *"He who has My commandments and keeps them, it is he who loves Me. And he who loves Me will be loved by My Father, and I will love him and manifest Myself to him." (John 14:21)*

The Book of Life says that we are not true Christians because:
• we do not have love and care for people
• we do not focus on the Word of God
• our attitudes and behaviours deny the Lord.

Care is totally based on love. Thus, without love, it will be very difficult for us to demonstrate the kind of care to others who may be in need of help. Moreover, it is very important for us to understand that there is no way that people only need our help when we are totally free and ready to assist: it is impossible. Therefore, we should be aware that others need our help, our presence or our time, just when we are very busy doing other things, just as the first two men in the Bible passage were very busy travelling somewhere to do their work. Furthermore, at the time when we are entangled with activities, or facing problems or difficulties, our decision-making will prove whether we are true Christians or not. It is at this moment that the King of kings is interested in our decision.

We base our lives on faith, love and sharing, and not by being spiritual people. This is because the Bible asks us to love one another as our Lord loves us. Through this love, we can share and help one another to glorify the name of our Father. By doing these, we will open doors to our success, and, as a result, our Father's name will be praised.

Going to church involves so many things, and implies that we will carry the same cross of the Lord. Before we can do that, we must love with heart-commitment and not just mental love, as many believers do. We love people in different ways, compared with the love the Bible talks about. Carrying the same cross as the Lord involves total life-sacrifice for other people, without compensation, payment or the intention to receive anything.

The Bible says that we Christians have to share problems, joy and mourning with one another. Sharing problems is the most difficult, and is the major bottleneck of our spiritual growth and development in this world. Why? Sharing problems with each other is based on love and care that brings a strong relationship. This loving relationship is the heart of Christianity. It indicates that we are clinging to the cross, the beauty of care and the true image of God in that person.

The Bible clearly states that we must have fellowship with one another. This fellowship is about joining together to form one body. However, today Christians and churches of God lack this. We do not want to unite with others, because we are more interested in our own affairs rather than that of others. Have we understood the meaning and importance of fellowship that our Lord is asking us to have? The fellowship our Lord mentions is not only about communing with

God and walking in His truth, or associating with other Christians on religious matters. Sometimes it involves physical help, aiding one another in times of problems, or digging deep into our wallets and purses to solve the problems of our brothers or sisters. This kind of fellowship is not about financial matters, but is based on love; it shows how kind and compassionate we can be to one another. This fellowship goes beyond our relationship to the public.

Fellowship is the basis for the signs of hope for Christians who are in the body of Christ and who work to extend God's Kingdom. This is not financial or physical, but loves from our hearts and minds.

This Christian sharing is a difficult issue for the body of Christ to face and discuss, for we cannot even relate in love with each other. How much more can we relate in love with other people, to proclaim Lord's rule of peace, healing and the new life of our His teachings? In fact, the burden of this issue causes destruction in the body of Christ. It limits our spiritual growth and contributes to the denial of our Lord Jesus Christ. Also, it discourages backsliders even more, makes unbelievers unhappy and distracts them from joining the body of Christ.

Causes of the Decline of Christian Spiritual Growth

These are the main causes:
• wrong interpretation of Christ's career and His teachings
• lack of understanding and wrong application of the Bible message
• no heart-commitment to the Word
• no loving care for people
• no loving relationship or fellowship
• more focus on finance and property than on the Word of God.

It is very important for all of us to know that fellowship is the main heart of Christianity. It lets us be the fruit of the religion and proclaim the Gospel of Christ. Our failure and that of all the churches of Christ to unite as one body of Christ, so that we might achieve His teachings and have our burdens carried by Him on the cross – all of this has a damaging effect on the aspirations of all well-run and ambitious Christian institutions.

8 Giving

Introduction

A loving response from one person to another often involves giving something. A gift with a willing heart is valuable and is therefore appreciated by the receiver, who thanks the giver to show appreciation. Giving shows how people are important to us, how we can get close to them, and help open opportunities for both of us. This chapter is about the classification and importance of giving, and the motives for it. It also gives some common examples of giving in the church of God that are meaningless and not useful.

Defining Giving

Giving is when something is offered to someone as a present that will benefit them. This type of gift is non-spiritual; it deals with worldly things instead of spiritual things. In every example of success, there is support, and a present acts as support for people to restore or regain strength to continue their life. If this kind of present is given to the church, it gives the church support for it to move on. However, it is not given to needy people, to make their situation worse, neither is it given to a church to receive something in return.

Every gift has a motive, which is even more important than the gift. Whether we know the giver or not, it engrosses our mind, since the motive behind the gift is the key to the giver's blessings. The motive behind giving determines the type of reward that may be received.

Gifts might be: money, clothes, care, shelter, helps to solve problems, good advice and encouragement, teaching, and time for others.

Here are some types of giving in the Bible: the willing giving by Abraham, who offered his only son (*Genesis 22:1-19*); the voluntary giving by Zacchaeus, who gave his goods to feed the poor without being asked (*Luke 19:1-9*); and the 'reward giving' by those who give to be seen by others, but who have their only reward here on earth (*Matthew 6:2*). In the Old Testament, *Deuteronomy 15:10* says, *You shall surely give to him, and your heart should not be grieved when you give to him, because for this thing the LORD your God will bless you in all your works and in all to which you put your hand.*

Giving in the book of Acts involves many things, not only money. Furthermore, it encourages us to help one another. The Bible does not tell us to give with the intention of receiving money or more that we give, but says that it is more blessed to give. Nor does it say that we will get any reward; blessings will come from the Lord, and through others. Giving is a response to the self-giving of the Lord Jesus Christ for us.

Types of Giving

He looked up and saw the rich putting their gifts into the treasury, and He saw also a certain poor widow putting in two mites. So He said, "Truly I say to you that this poor widow has put in more than all; for all these out of their abundance have put in offerings for God, but she out of her poverty put in all the livelihood that she had." (Luke 21:1–4)

There were two gifts – one from rich people and the other from a poor widow. These demonstrate the two kinds of gifts: giving out of abundance, and out of poverty giving our livelihood. An offering is a contribution or a gift, to the Church, for a special purpose. The rich people did not give from their heart, compared with the poor widow, since maybe they thought that the money was going to be used for Temple work, and as a result, they would not benefit from it. They were more interested in their own business than in the business of God. So, despite their riches, they were not interested in contributing and gave whatever they wished.

Livelihood is what is needed to support life. Therefore, out of her poverty, the poor woman emptied herself and gave all she had to cater for herself and her family, to be used for God's work. She gave to God with a free heart, without thinking about what she would receive, and without any influence. She was much more concerned about the Temple than about her own life.

This shows us that giving is not what we give: it is what comes from the heart. This is why the poor widow was recognised by Jesus as one who gave her best, by putting in more than the rich person. Some people give gifts which are not from their heart, but because of some other circumstances. This type of giving may not do the giver any good. It is not necessarily the amount, quality or quantity of the gifts that is important: it is the real motive behind the gift that shows its importance.

There are two main types of giving: non-spiritual and spiritual. Non-spiritual giving does not deal with spiritual things, but has to do with our physical human life.

Genuine Giving

And Moses spoke to all the congregation of the children of Israel, saying, "This is the thing which the Lord commanded, saying: 'Take from among you an offering to the Lord. Whoever is of a willing heart, let him bring it as an offering to the Lord: gold, silver and bronze; blue, purple, and scarlet thread, fine linen, and goats' hair'." (Exodus 35:4–6)

Then everyone came whose heart was stirred, and everyone whose spirit was willing, and they brought the Lord's offering for the work of the tabernacle of meeting, for all its service, and for the holy garments. (Exodus 35:21)

This type of giving is a gift with neither pay nor bribe. It is freely given, with no intention of receiving anything. The gift is anything that is beneficial to the people in need. The genuine gift that the Bible talks about is a gift that does not depend on how much we have to give, but on whole-hearted love.

Merits of Giving

There are advantages to genuine giving with a free heart. Giving does the following:
• it opens doors to Gospel blessings
• it helps the power of God be manifest
• it proclaims the Gospel through loving and caring for others
• it demonstrates love
• it brings joy and peace
• it makes the worship of God very easy and flexible
• it brings a better relationship between the giver and the receiver
• it is the most important factor in winning souls.

Giving from Wrong Motives

He who sows sparingly will also reap sparingly, and he who sows bountifully will also reap bountifully. So let each one give as he purposes in his heart, not grudgingly or of necessity; for God loves a cheerful giver. (2 Corinthians 9: 6–7)

Giving from wrong motives is a type of gift with the intention of receiving something back, or a bribe. It can be caused by a lack of understanding. With this type of giving, it is only we, the givers, who know what we are doing. The gift is not given freely. These gifts are conditional and are not based on love. Moreover, this type of giving has nothing to do with the Word of God, but rather with worldly goods.

The more you give, the more you will be blessed: this has become our philosophy now in the body of Christ. The more money we give to our church or needy people, the more we will be blessed by God. It implies that if we do not have more money to give to our Father's Kingdom or needy people, He who created us is not going to bless us; if we give less compared with those who are able to give more, we will receive small blessings from our Father. And if we do not have money to give, the Lord will not bless us. In fact, many of us now believe this philosophy.

The superior modern system of donation-giving that has come into the kingdom of God from nowhere is a growing concern, since it destroys our worshipping of God, and creates many problems in the Kingdom of God. In particular, the worship of the King of kings is not possible for poor Christians. Furthermore, unbelievers and backsliders find it very difficult and confusing to come and worship our Maker with us.

We have to ask ourselves if the Bible says that the more we give to the Kingdom of God or needy people, the more we will be blessed. The Bible does not say this. Giving anything to God's Kingdom or to people, with the intention of receiving something back, is an indirect bribe or indirect stealing.

An *indirect bribe* is offering any substance or reward to somebody to do something. Doing this is an indirect bribe because we want others to do something for us. We may think that it is wrong or that they would not do it, so we offer a gift to open a way. Indirect stealing means taking something dishonestly. We want to take something, yet we don't want others to see or know. We give them something to show that we truly love and care for them, which we definitely do not.

What we do now – is it different from indirect bribes and stealing? There is no difference. The things we give are not given freely from our hearts, but to influence our Maker to bless us or to get more from Him.

According to the book of 2 Corinthians 9:7, "let each one give as he purposes in his heart, not grudgingly or of necessity; for God loves a cheerful giver."

Again, we give our substance, not according to our abilities and possessions as the Bible says, but to get something ourselves. When we give money to the Kingdom of God, we do it to obtain more interest from the money we give. So, is it any different from investing money in a bank to get more interest? We invest our money in a bank in order to get more interest from time to time than the initial investment. Is the Kingdom of God a bank? It may be a bank for us to invest our lives, so that we may have everlasting life in the future. However, it is not a bank for us to invest money in, with the intention of receiving more than we give.

The Bible tells that if we give to the church or needy people, then we will be blessed. However, it does not say how or how much we will be blessed. Furthermore, it does not tell us, for example, that if we invest or give a thousand pounds freely from our heart to support our church or needy people, then we will get twice that amount back, or less from it, as some of us interpret the Bible message. We have to ask ourselves whether we are doing the same now in the Kingdom of God as investing our money in the bank to gain more interest.

Some of us so-called born-again Christians think that we are wiser than our Maker. Could we steal from our King of kings who created all things, or bribe Him? We will not get blessings from our God, just because of all the money or substances that we give to His Kingdom. Have we asked ourselves the reason why we are not blessed?

Reasons for not getting Blessings from Giving

Giving is one of the basic roots of the Gospel. It promotes good relationships and opens a way for blessings. However, here are some reasons that can block these blessings, despite what we give to needy people:

- we do not deeply understand the Bible and giving, so we give wrongly
- we do not know the substances we can offer to needy people as a gift
- the money we give is not given freely to the Kingdom of God or to needy people
- we do not give according to our abilities and possessions
- we give with the intention of receiving something back.

Most of us can financially help needy people in our families, but we do not want to do so. Why? Is it because the people will not appreciate it? The reason is that we think that if we give our money to the church, with the intention of receiving more from it, we will get financial blessings from God, rather than helping or giving the money to needy people in our families, or poor people we know.

Do our gifts to the church go to the Lord instead of going to needy or poor people? Does our God of the universe, who created all things, need our money? Does the Bible say that if we give money to the church with the intention of getting more, and forget needy people or poor people in our families, we will be blessed? This is why we are suffering now, despite all the money we give to God's Kingdom. We simply do not know the God we worship, and we do not bother to know Him, because we look for physical rather than spiritual things.

Also, the giving that the Bible refers to does not apply to money only, as many of us think it does. It applies to any help that we can give to any human beings: food, clothing, good advice, problem-solving, encouragement and teaching. This help must come from the heart, with no intention of receiving. Nowhere does the Book of Life say that the more we bless people who need help or give to people who need it, with the intention of receiving from it, the more we will be blessed.

Giving, especially money, to help needy people, but not freely from our hearts but rather with the intention of receiving more, is better than not giving at all, because it is not forced. Giving depends on what we have and our willingness to give, that comes freely from the heart – this is the vital key to receiving blessings back from your giving. The blessings we receive from giving, that are mentioned in the Bible – this does not mean that we will only be blessed if we give to God's Kingdom. It also applies to blessing needy people with our gifts. Giving to needy people or the church of God does not mean that we will be only blessed with money, as some of us think. Blessings will come from God, who knows what we need in our individual lives. Also, in the normal sense, God does not need our giving in order to bless us. We are His children, therefore He always cares for us, protects and comforts us freely, as we care freely for our children. What do we have to give to Our Father, who possesses everything? What does God lack and need from His poor children? He created all things, both in Heaven and on earth, before He blesses.

The church itself needs money to pay bills, purchase materials for the church building, pay pastors and all those who help, in order for the body of Christ to function. Also, as a church, we children of God believe and are entrusted to pay our tithes to God, and bring in our offerings as a measure of our appreciation and gratitude to our Father. If we are charged for our salvation given to us by God, obviously we can never pay. However, through His love for us, we have to bring in our substance, according to the words in the Bible:

Every man shall give as he is able (Deuteronomy 16:17)
Bring all the tithes into the storehouse, that there may be food in My house.
(Malachi 3:8–12)
And all the tithe of the land…is the Lord's. (Leviticus27:30)

However, this does not say that the Bible says that the more we give, the more God will bless us.

Ignoring our Brothers and Sisters in Need

In need means that something is lacking that is required for our welfare, such as money and food. It might be lacking because of poverty or sickness. Ignoring our brothers and sisters in need means that we turn our backs on our brothers, sisters, parents or suffering people, especially those whom we know, and give our substance to the church in order to receive blessings.

This way of giving has become a pattern, to the extent that we ignore our brothers and sisters. It illustrates the importance of people, and shows us that it is not our gifts to the church that show that we are doing Gospel work. Doing the work of the Gospel of

Christ is not in church, neither is it giving our money to the church. Anything that happens in the church is the church activity, which contributes to our development as well as helping the church to move on. The work of Jesus Christ's Gospel is caring for others, based on love and nothing else, If we are definitely aware of those we know in need, but we ignore them and give our money to the church, then what is the point of being disciples of Christ and the Gospel, whose main key is love ?

Is it right to ignore our brothers and sisters who are starving at home or who need our assistance at home, in our communities and societies, and give our money to the kingdom of God in order to receive blessings? Does the Bible recommend us to do this? The Bible recommends that churches use the money, and give these donations to needy people.

All these wrong motives for giving contribute brutally to the denying of our Lord Jesus Christ, since we have no deep understanding of the Bible, and do not bother to understand it. As a result, born-again Christians face so many problems these days, and believers are backsliding. Everyone will bear witness that without Christian assistance to go deeply into the Bible and to adopt methods to get rid of all unworthy things, the churches of Christ will struggle to function in future.

The effects of giving from wrong motives are seen when we:
• seize the power of God
• eliminate poor Christians from the church
• recognise only rich Christians
• have no love, joy and peace
• make worshipping God very difficult
• use the church for personal affairs
• use the name of God in vain
• chase worldly goods rather than the Gospel
• have more woes and no healing.

Generous Giving

He who sows sparingly will also reap sparingly, and he who sows bountifully will also reap bountifully. So let each one give as he purposes in his heart, not grudgingly or of necessity; for God loves a cheerful giver. (2 Corinthians 9: 6–7)

As believers in Christ, it is essential for us to examine these words, since they are commonly used in services of worship during offertory time.

Generous means selfless, and in terms of giving, means more than enough. Giving generously means we give more than enough, rather than being selfish. Love is not mentioned; neither does it say that the gifts are freely given. If the motive behind giving is not based on love and it does not come from heart freely, then the gift has a wrong motive. It does not matter whether our gift is bounteous or generous; what matters most here is the motive behind the gift, because the motive for giving deters the type of reward.

Giving freely from the heart is not the same as giving generously. The issue of giving generously is an indirect way of forcing both rich and poor Christians to give money to the church. Many of us constantly dip into our pockets for the crises facing poor people across the world. We have now set our sights on charity work that will save lives. In fact, this is one of our tasks. We are committed to using church property and money wisely and well, and reporting back to others on what has been achieved. We always help people who are in trouble, through poverty or poor health, to rebuild their lives. Our goals are to double the amount of aid and eliminate the poverty and sadness of people, by helping them through various means and letting them know the God we worship. However, if church property or people's contributions are used for other things, with no accountability, what will happen to the contributions for the crisis?

We should be aware that not all gifts have blessings. Some gifts we give are worthless. If the motives behind many gifts are examined, it is not much better than giving nothing. So many gifts have been given to the Kingdom of God or to needy people, but nothing good has come from the gifts, though they might have benefited the recipients. Most of our gifts are based on wrong motives, since want the church to give us attention, instead of us dedicating ourselves to the Gospel.

We underestimate the willingness and tremendous work of Jesus Christ, and we mislead people. We are intentionally or unintentionally creating obstacles to the Gospel, to dominate the world and put people's lives at risk.

We have to understand that the Gospel is not about giving to the church, or forcing people to give more to the church in order to be blessed by God, neither is it in ignoring our brothers and sisters who we know we are in need, and giving so that God will bless us. Moreover, it is not the great music and instruments in the church, though they make the worship attractive and enjoyable. The worshipping of God is our heart's commitment to the Lord. The Lord requires our total and unconditional worship. Our Lord wants us to give ourselves totally to Him while looking at all that is going on in the world. He is the chief cornerstone in our lives, so He takes every care of us. As time goes by, the world is getting tougher and tougher. There is no doubt that things of the world are not going to become easier and more favourable for us. This indicates that the time of our Lord's second coming is getting near. So, it will be necessary for us, God's disciples, to stand fast and continue to declare the love, care, joy and peace of the Lord to His world at large.

In fact, God's deathless love has made us more than conquerors and has scattered all our fears and gloom. Therefore, we have to be straightforward believers, and put malpractices and confusion into the right channels, to protect our lives and the Gospel, and promote the Gospel as well.

The Book of Life definitely assures us that there is life after death. So we need not worry about worldly things, but rather open our minds and our hearts, to believe in and accept Christ, and walk with Him with an open heart.

9 Gospel Threats

Introduction

An important requirement for the Bible is that it should be used, taught and interpreted genuinely. Nothing should be added to or taken from it. Teaching should be the outcome of the Bible, since we will be affected by this teaching. If it is wrong or not biblical, then it will have a negative effect as well as a positive one. This has three aspects: effects on the Gospel, on us and on the world at large. This chapter deals with the use of the Bible and such teaching, and how our overall response has an effect on the lives of other people.

Threats

A *threat* refers to something that people do to hurt others in order to gain something. People create danger for others, because they oppose rules and regulations. Doing unacceptable things leads to the destruction of lives. This threat means real danger, if people sit back and do not stand against these dangerous behaviours. What we do may damage the entire body of Christ, and the lives of God's people will be lost.

Gospel threats are the way in which the world threatens the Gospel, the story of Jesus Christ and His teachings. Some things that we do in the body of Christ may also be contrary to God's Word. These things threaten the Gospel and the people of God. In fact, they have a huge negative impact on the Gospel, since they stunt the advancement of God's Kingdom throughout the world.

The Gospel of Christ is recognised as one of the best religions in the world and has a strong reputation for worship. However, ridiculous attitudes and behaviour of believers are getting out of hand.

Some church leaders register the church as a charity, but they don't do charity work. Why are they doing that? What are the main purposes of a church? Do we donate money to these churches so that the church will do charity work? Where do these donations go?

We believe that God builds His church through human beings. So, the church belongs to us and is not personal property.

Every day of worship, huge numbers of unbelievers come to the body of Christ and want to stay. This indicates that Christianity is safe and is one of the best religions on this planet. Therefore, we, the disciples of Christ, should be proud of it. We should show that the Gospel of Christ is about worshipping God. This is based on love and care for others, rather than using the name of God to obtain personal property through lying and corruption.

As we are hungry for the Gospel every day, Satan indirectly threatens the Gospel by using money as a weapon, in order to thwart it to accomplish his objectives. In fact, Satan knows that there is no better influence on us than money. It was money that was used by the same Satan, in three occasions in the Bible, to terminate the ministry of our Lord Jesus Christ, two thousand years ago.

So they watched Him, and sent spies who pretended to be righteous, that they might seize on His words, in order to deliver Him to the power and the authority of the governor. Then they asked Him, saying, "Teacher, we know that you say and teach rightly, and you do not show personal favouritism, but teach the way of God in truth: Is it lawful for us to pay taxes to Caesar or not?"

But He perceived their craftiness, and said to them, "Why do you test Me? Show Me a denarius. Whose image and inscription does it have?"

They answered and said, "Caesar's"

And He said to them, "Render therefore to Caesar the things that are Caesar's, and to God the things that are God's." (Luke20:20–25)

He found in the temple those who sold oxen and sheep and doves, and the moneychangers doing business.

When He had made a whip of cords, He drove them all out of the temple, with the sheep and the oxen, and poured out the changers' money and overturned the tables. And He said to those who sold doves, "Take these things away! Do not make My Father's house a house of merchandise!" (John 2:13-16)

Then one of the twelve, called Judas Iscariot, went to the chief priests and said, "What are you willing to give me if I deliver Him to you?" And they counted out to him thirty pieces of silver. So from that time he sought opportunity to betray Him. (Matthew 26: 14–16)

It is clear here that Satan used money on three occasions as a weapon to terminate Christ's life and His ministry. On the first occasion, the people watched the Lord and sent spies who pretended to be righteous, that they might seize upon the work of Christ, in order to deliver Him to the power and authority of the governor at that time.

We must be alert in every situation of dishonesty because of the threat from Satan, as the Bible warns us. The Bible urges us to be extra vigilant, to keep watch and keep away from these people, since they are the agents of Satan. They are on a mission to see who the most likely members for Satan's kingdom are. Therefore, this issue should continue to concern us. Certainly, they need church, to preach and convince people to support them, for they intend to take large numbers from the body of Christ.

Why does God assure us about the coming of these false Christians? Is He not the head of His church? Is He not going to deal with these people? The Lord Himself tells us not to underestimate these people, even though He knows everything and He is always in control, taking care of His church and us.

We believe that it is wrong to speak out on unacceptable matters in the body of Christ. Some even think that if we step in, God will take our lives from us. However, the proverb says 'charity begins at home'. As Christians, we must let our yes be yes and our no be no. We have to be straightforward, because we worship God, who is the Maker of all things, not human beings like us.

The Bible reminds us to be genuine Christians, not hypocrites.

Where will we start, in correcting our mistakes? Is it from our churches and homes, or from outside? Being true Christians – is it about reading and quoting from the Bible? Have we asked ourselves the reason why we have to be genuine Christians? It is of vital importance to point out all wrong matters in the church and put them right. If we do not speak out and deal with them, it will put the Gospel and believers at risk. As disciples of Christ, how do we classify ourselves – as hypocritical or as genuine Christians?

We should note that no two days are the same. As time goes on, we will experience all sorts of problems. Being believers, born-again and Spirit-filled, when a problem arises, there will be time to think about the problem and solve it. It is our duty and responsibility to analyse problems in the body of Christ and solve them. Solving the problems day in and day out will drive us toward our aims and make us feel proud. Honestly, it is not going to be easy. Yet, as far as we have decided to carry the cross of Calvary, we have to press on all the time, to achieve our aims of being Christians.

Money as a Heart

Money is legal tender that is accepted as a medium of exchange. This legal tender includes bank notes and coins of the realm, made up of silver, gold or other metal or paper, for use commercially or for making payment. It is a government-authorised public body that issues this kind of money. It cannot be refused when offered as payment. In fact, the number of bank notes is unlimited; however, the use of the coins is controlled in accordance with their value.

The money that Satan uses to damage the Gospel of Christ and His followers is described here in this book as 'the heart of human beings'.

A heart pumps blood to all parts of the body by contracting and expanding, to enable us to sustain life. Failure of this heart to function well will result in death; therefore, we totally depend on our heart.

The heart is also named when we feel, hate, love, and desire.

This book describes money as a human's heart because we all need money to purchase necessities – water, food, clothing and shelter, to sustain our life. Without money, it is reasonable to doubt whether we can survive in this world full of woes. It is clear that money can do all things, and with it, impossible things become possible. Without money, we become like a dead body.

We focus on obtaining this money, without any consideration for the means of getting it or its effects. We are determined to be rich. This is not a bad thing, since we have authority and possess all things.

However, the means of getting this money is unacceptable. As a result, the purpose of Christianity is lost,
and the ways to obtain it are closed to us.

Purpose of the Gospel

The main purpose of the Gospel of Christ is to save people's lives from Satan. How can this be achieved?

It is amazing that most of us do not have a clue about the weapons that we must use to proclaim the Gospel. Also, we do not know that the proclamation of the Gospel is the only way to let the public know and come to Christ, for their lives to be saved forever.

It is common knowledge that Jesus Christ came to this world two thousand years ago, to die on the cross and save the lives of all children of God. This amazing work of Christ indicates that we are all entitled to these benefits. The Book of Life also tells us that to obtain this free gift, we have some conditions to fulfil.

What are these conditions and their significance? We can only proclaim the Gospel of Christ if we know our identity and destiny. Who are we, where do we come from, what have we become, and where will we go at the end? To be able to assess ourselves and focus on our objectives, it is vital to know our position in Christ, always forget the past, and concentrate on the present. Having done all these, then it is important to know and understand the key weapons to be used to achieve our objectives.

It is no surprise that we are abusing the Gospel of Christ. Why? Because we do not know the key weapons we have to use to proclaim the Gospel. Those of us who know them may not deeply understand how to use these weapons. Really, it is sad to say that many born-again, Spirit-filled Christians do not have the master keys of the Gospel. They are not able to proclaim the Gospel to save people's lives, even though they always do preach the Gospel. To be able to save people's lives by proclaiming the Gospel, they must have love and care for people.

The proclamation of the Gospel is not always going to church, reading the Bible, quoting from the Bible and preaching the Gospel to thousands of people every day. Doing this will equip us and remind us that we are members of a society. Are we doing Christian work to fulfil the objectives of the Gospel?

Key Weapons to Proclaim the Gospel

The key weapons to proclaim the Gospel are the things that enable us to fulfil our Gospel ambition: what we should do in order to become followers of Christ, which is considered to be the inheritance of Christ, and to influence others in the world.

Love and care are the key weapons to assist us in proclaiming the Gospel of Jesus Christ, after having concrete faith in our God in all our doings. The proclamation of the Gospel has nothing to do with faith. What matters and is taken into account here is love and care. The public want to know that Jesus Christ loves us and cares for us, so it is this love and care for all people that influence people to approach Christ. They want to see whether we have this kind of love and care, since this will demonstrate the kind of God we worship. However, they do not want to see whether we have faith in our God or in the words we speak.

We should know that, without love and care for people, the proclamation of the Gospel can never be achieved, even though we have faith in all our doings. Every day, many new members will come to the body of Christ by various means. All the time, many come to

Christ, or come and are born again. However, in the long run they will vanish or backslide. How many people are still in the body of Christ, out of those who came to know Christ in our church? What has happened to these vanished people? What is going on in the church? Is there any problem? If so, what are the causes of these issues? How will we solve them? One out of every hundred Christians will have time to analyse this problem, since others do not have love and care for people. They do not even want to see us or know about our situation, but wish us to be always in church, to give our donation.

We are battling and hungry to get people to come to the body of Christ, while true love and care for them are not there. We preach the Bible and witness to the Gospel of Christ, thinking that doing these things is the main job of proclaiming the Gospel, rather than studying the footsteps of Christ. Jesus Christ did not proclaim the Gospel by spiritual reading and preaching. He proclaimed the Gospel by physical demonstration of His love and care for people. His attitudes and behaviour proved to the public that He was and is the Messiah. Jesus Christ, the King of kings, did not influence the public to follow Him; people chose and accepted Him as their Messiah, through His true nature of love and care for people.

Frankly, it is this love and care for others that opened all locked doors for Him to achieve His mission. Our Lord knew that without love and care for others, it would be impossible for His disciples to achieve the objectives of the Gospel. Otherwise, why, in the Bible, did he keep telling us to love one another and have care for others? We should be aware that the proclamation of the Gospel has nothing to do with wonders and miracles. We gear up and queue up for wonders and miracles, thinking that they are the major keys to proclaim the Gospel. These wonders and miracles are the fruits of the Gospel; before these fruits can be manifest, they need the ingredients, which are love and care. Wonders and miracles are evidence of the power of the Word of God. Without evidence of power, God's words become of no use. Nowhere does the Bible tell us that we can proclaim the Gospel with faith. It is necessary for us to note this. Most of us think that if we have faith in the Word of the Lord that is all: whatever we wish for will come true. We do not understand that the key words to perform all these things are love and care. Does it work if we go out with faith to witness, so that someone will come to the kingdom of God, while we do not talk to our parents, friends or our neighbours? This is the main reason why the churches of God are still empty, despite all the means of proclaiming the Gospel.

The churches are full of sick people and all sorts of problems. This is why we are always keen for the power of God to heal deaf, lame and blind people, and to perform wonders and miracles. Yet we do not experience anything and nothing is happening in the churches, as we expect it should. This is because we depend on faith to spread the Gospel and perform wonders and miracles. It should not be so, because faith is divine protection for physical factors through God's direct intervention. Love and care are the Gospel roots that we lack, and the lack of these drives us away from our objectives. As more people pour into the church, the more people become backsliders or return to the world. Knowing our weakness, Satan uses wonders and miracles to influence us and lead us away from achieving our objectives.

Satan is multiplying his agents, to come into the body of Christ by means of performing wonders and miracles. These people pretend to be born-again, Spirit-filled Christians. They rush into the church of God to take the top positions, so that they can easily mislead believers. However, worshipping God has nothing to do with acquiring position. While we forget the key weapons to guard us in every situation, we have no chance of standing with the Gospel, rather than following the world.

Christian Lives of Luxury

Rich oppressors will be judged:

Come now, you rich, weep and howl for your miseries that are coming upon you! Your riches are corrupted, and your garments are moth-eaten. Your gold and silver are corroded, and their corrosion will be a witness against you and will eat your flesh like fire. You have heaped up treasure in the last days. Indeed the wages of the labourers who mowed your fields, which you kept back by fraud, cry out; and the cries of the reapers have reached the ears of the Lord of Sabaoth. You have lived on the earth in pleasure and luxury; you have fattened your hearts as in a day of slaughter. You have condemned, you have murdered the just; he does not resist you. (James 5: 1–6)

Luxury is riches or wealth. To live in luxury is to be rich; everybody on this earth looks forward to this. The Bible sets out the responsibilities of rich people, in the book of *1 Timothy 6: 17–19*:

Command those who are rich in this present age not to be haughty, nor to trust in uncertain riches but in the living God, who gives us richly all things to enjoy. Let them do good, that they be rich in good works, ready to give, willing to share, storing up for themselves a good foundation for the time to come, that they may lay hold on eternal life.

However, the means or results of riches are a different thing. It is not wrong to be rich, neither is it condemned by the teachings of Jesus Christ. The problem arises when some of us become rich and we consider poor people to be nothing. Sadly, we forget that we were nothing before.

Some use devious means to become wealthy and misuse other people in order to obtain whatever they want. Not all rich people use wrong methods to make money; not all give aid and comfort others. Many do respect other people, regardless of circumstance. This chapter describes their wealthy lives, and the use of church money or property by some Christians; it shows its effects on the Gospel as well as on the people of God.

The term *'Christian lives of luxury'* is used to describe our wealthy living conditions, as people starve around the world. It is beyond what is really necessary, and beyond biblical requirements. Many of us today, especially church leaders, live in luxury, while others are starving. Many church leaders use the Gospel to make enough money for them to live in comfort. We save some money, especially church money, for luxuries. Luxuries are pleasant but are not necessary, since people are starving to death. Is it necessary, or important, to save money, while other people are dying of sickness, hunger, starvation or poverty? It is not surprising that, even within the same body of Christ, some Christians are dying of poverty, while the church does not use its money to save the lives of these people, or invest it in order to contribute to their lives in the future.

It is surprising and unbelievable that we, the disciples of Jesus Christ, make ourselves richer, day in and day out, by exploiting Christians and the public in God's name. We call ourselves disciples of Jesus Christ, and use the name of the Lord without even thinking about its effects on the Gospel and people's lives.

It is not wrong for us or the entire church to do business. However, some leaders use God's name to influence people, to take people's money and property to make themselves rich. These people are cruel and unjust, especially to their fellow Christians. However, because they use the Gospel of Christ as a means of gaining their personal achievement, it is difficult to identify them. Such people are corrupt, doubtlessly, and will be dealt with as stated above in the book of James 5: 1–6, since these kinds of Christians are false or bogus Christians.

It is good to make money through genuine business, but not by using almighty God's name to proclaim the Gospel to achieve our personal objective. We do not even notice that it will have an effect on the Gospel, or care that it will damage Christianity and people's lives. If it is right to use Jesus Christ's church as a commercial placed to cheat people to get rich, what is the difference between doing church business and a drugs business? Do we not have the same objective, of getting money at the end of the day? Because of the pressure of acquiring money in this world, we are totally confused and full of mistrust.

It is very disturbing to see that so-called born-again Spirit-filled Christians use our Lord Jesus Christ's church as a business, to damage the Gospel and put people's life at risk, instead of using it to proclaim the true Gospel to save people's lives. In the first place, this kind of business should not take place in the church at all. In the second place, people are donating their money to help and take care of needy people. Where do these donations go?

The world is full of prostitution, poverty, poor health and high death rates, all of which are increasing. Many of us are shocked by this, but many of us do not care or want to know the causes of these problems. The cause is likely to be poverty.

As believers, it is our concern to donate money, help create jobs, and assist these people. It is very bad news for us to get richer through people's donations to the church, keeping thousands of pounds (or other currency), while millions of people in other parts of the world lose their lives because of poverty.

In fact, there are many questions to ask ourselves as believers, such as why people are born to be prostitutes, to starve or to die? Whose is the responsibility? The Bible shows us that to be true disciples of Christ, we have to carry the Cross of Calvary, as our Lord did. This does not mean enjoying ourselves at church or at home, or enjoying ourselves through donations to the church or charity work. We must not use church money for personal affairs, nor call ourselves Christians, while our brothers and sisters are dying over there.

We are obliged to follow in the footsteps of Christ and fulfil our role in the Gospel. Jesus Christ came to save all human beings' lives from the hands of Satan. He did have love and care for all people, and He was not a hypocritical Messiah. However, He asks us to follow Him by carrying His Cross. It is our duty and responsibility to do the same thing as Him, since that is the only way we can become His disciples and proclaim the Gospel. This Gospel is based on love and care for other people according to their needs, to save their lives. We can do all these things, by going out there to assist these needy people and not confining ourselves to one place. Also, exploiting people to take their money and property by any means cannot make us true disciples.

Look at Christ's life and His ministry. Did the Maker of everything stay in one place to proclaim the Gospel? Did He use His power to monopolise people or influence people, to take their worldly goods, like money and property?

False Christians

Then if anyone says to you, "Look, here is the Christ!" or "There!" do not believe it. For false Christs and false prophets will rise and show great signs and wonders to deceive, if possible, even the elect. (Matthew 24: 23–4)

False Christians are people who claim to be followers of Jesus Christ, but are not. Their true colours are shown by their behaviour.

At times, it is really difficult to notice it, since they often use the Gospel in every aspect of their activities. They use the Gospel as their weapon of success, to camouflage themselves and cover what they do. They definitely understand that it is only by doing this that they can achieve their aims. This raises some questions about who is responsible for them, who pays the price of such Christians, and what happens if such Christians are exposed.

Every day now, we, the disciples of Jesus Christ of Bethlehem, work harder than in previous years to provide for our churches and do church charity work efficiently and effectively. The demand for our work and donations means love and care for people and the ability to help needy people around the world. Many of us struggle to balance work with church and home responsibilities. Many of us work long hours and work overtime, to provide the best help to the church of God to do Christian work. However, as born-again, Spirit-filled Christians, we use the church of Christ for personal business. We embezzle church funds for needy people, and this defamation of Jesus Christ's name increases constantly. We get confused and discouraged about whether to keep on holding to Christ or not, because of what church leaders and other Christians do with people's donations. These donors may not even have enough money for their own needs, but contribute to the church's charity work, in order to save the lives of people around the world in Christ's name.

However, those who think they have dominion over the church use it as their commercial ground. Sometimes, it seems that, without worth, we cannot go to church. However, going to church to worship God in reality has nothing to do with having property or income. In fact, the Bible shows us that, in the body of Christ, no one is worthless. However, now it is the opposite: going to church and worshipping God now depend on money.

So, what do we do about these people who pollute the Gospel? Are we going to let them go on with these behaviours until Christ comes? The book of Matthew assures us that there will be false Christians in the last days. These false or bogus Christians turn the Gospel around, and cannot be trusted. If we keep quiet without stepping in, throwing them out, and putting things right, then what is our role in Christianity? Are we true or hypocritical disciples?
It appears that no one in God's Kingdom is allowed to offer differing views, except those few people who are in charge of the church. It is not surprising that believers' angry opinions about malpractices in the Kingdom of God are not going to be aired, and that no action is taken. It really seems that there will be no tidy-up exercise to get rid of all these affairs, so believers' spiritual growth and the saving of people's lives will not happen, since the malpractices happen in the church. This means that, in the body of Christ, the children of God do not have a say.

In fact, if we classify ourselves as true disciples of Jesus Christ, it is our duty and responsibility to fight against these people and any other rulers of darkness, who are pouring into the church of God to cause disaster. In the long run, it damages the Gospel and it harms people's lives, especially those who suffer the most.

Jesus Christ came to save us from our sins and suffering. Real Christians begin with a deep understanding of Christ's life and teachings. Our fear of speaking out against these malpractices in the Kingdom of God will not drive us to glory.

We have to ask ourselves why this is happening in the body of Christ. Are these people's actions worthy? How do we feel, knowing that these malpractices are going on? It is very strange and sad that we refuse to put things right. We welcome these malpractices every day and now we are in a position where we cannot afford to do this anymore. There is no point in 'beating about the bush', because all these malpractices in the body of Christ are the work of Satan.

There are many eyewitness accounts about Satan's activities in the body of Christ, which obviously confirm the prophecy in the Gospel of Matthew. The worship of God is not easy and will not get easier. It is purely a matter of faith, truth and determination. Only a very few people benefit financially from the church, despite people's generous contributions. Therefore, there must be a massive change in the Christian worship system, and a decision that can bring about the most dramatic change, to structure worship and to restrict religious malpractices and activities. We are stranded and desperate because, apart from these issues, many things go on in the church that cannot stand and are just too much for us to bear. We are under great pressure to give our time to combat these crises. Turning our back on all these crises will not help solve the problem in God's Kingdom.

It seems we are very sorry about the birth and death of Jesus Christ, since these malpractices have a great effect on us and the Gospel, as well as discouraging the public from coming to Christ. It is worrying that we spend all our lives worshipping God with the objective of fulfilling our vision and mission. We spend much time to obtaining a solution to this issue. However, nothing good has come out of it because others are not with us at all. We may think that because the church is not our personal property, we do not need to care about its damage. Others also think that, if God is in control of His church, why should we worry about it?

The progress of Christianity these days lies with our ability to reform and improve its relationship with the public. At all times, we must put the stability and safety of the church first. What we really need to know is the identity of these people, since it is now very difficult to recognise genuine Christians. Without this, we will never co-operate with these people to get valuable mission experience to achieve our tasks. However, it is our duty and responsibility as a body to host a campaign to thwart these bogus Christian malpractices that damage the Gospel and individual Christians' lives.

We should not dwell on what is wrong in the body of Christ, but make our intentions clear to concentrate on the Lord Jesus Christ. We must do this and achieve our ambitions, rather than letting people irritate us and affect our worship by weakening our concentration. False or bogus believers' actions in the body of Christ have many effects, as detailed below. Compared with church leaders, we ordinary Christians suffer the worst, and no measures have been taken to deal with the crisis.

Effects of False Christians

National church organisations should play a major role in mobilising believers' opinions to help combat this tragedy. We see that false Christians:
- damage the entire body of Jesus Christ
- discourage believers and do not lead to believers' spiritual growth
- confuse unbelievers and drive away the power of God from us
- hold back our victory on the cross and it reduces the number of Christians.

Honouring Church Leaders

Let the elders who rule well be counted worthy of double honour, especially those who labour in the word and doctrine. For the Scripture says, "You shall not muzzle an ox while it treads out the grain," and, "The labourer is worthy of his wages." (1 Timothy 5: 17–18)

Honouring Christians means to respect Christians, especially church leaders, for their hard work. It shows their hard work, regardless of all sorts of Gospel problems and malpractices.

We always have something against some Christians, particularly church leaders, because of malpractices in the body of Christ. Leaders in the church, such as elders and pastors, see that many things are going wrong in the churches, and it seems that this does not concern them.

We are currently enjoying huge success in our witness to Christ, actively recruiting new members to join the body of Christ. Those in authority in the church take us through the Gospel, and at the same time place us in an awkward position regarding the taking of money from us. In the name of God, they put pressure on people, especially believers, to donate to the church for God's work. They dictate to us how to live our lives, yet are not willing to guide or assist us. Moreover, they do not want to take the responsibility of taking care of us, by offering training: not just teaching the Gospel, but also educating, providing jobs and solutions to our needs, as well as dealing with the public needs of backsliders and non-Christians.

The increasing numbers of dishonest Christians is fuelled by Satan, through the business of position and money in the church. We realise that these dishonest Christians want conflict, because they establish churches using their own initiative and resources. So, because they are self-employed, it is up to them to use the churches in the way they wish. They do not even want us to know that they have registered these churches as Christian churches, so we are obliged to go along with their rules and regulations.

It is unbelievable that, as the number of Christians is booming, the backsliding rate is also weighing it down, because of bad church affairs. Something must be done to stop them, for otherwise they will destroy the Gospel. Also, how many people will this affect? Who will take responsibility for this problem? How is this problem going to be tackled and when is it going to be solved? We need to make a big decision about the leaders, and we wish to see if people will speak about this matter.

Although there are so many malpractices in the body of Jesus Christ, still we must have faith in the church leaders, since some of our leaders are genuine. Signing on as church workers is very hard, yet some leaders do extraordinarily good jobs. It is important to understand that church leaders play an essential part in our society. They are the means whereby most of us perform our service of worship. Their services are considerable and cover a very wide area of Gospel activities; through their services, many lives can be saved from woe, and also church growth will be helped.

Church leaders are important spiritually, because they act as intermediaries between us and God. They provide a range of services to satisfy the spiritual needs of all types of people, from unbelievers and backsliders, to mature Christians. We should realise that a genuine leadership system is vital, because it permits worship to be flexible and at a reasonable cost in the world at large, which is a considerable contribution to lives, economies and communities. Some leaders understand that worship of the God of Abraham, Isaac and Jacob, and the Gospel, is not to be taken lightly.

Despite all the problems in the churches where we worship, we continue holding on to Christ and standing for Him, to protect the Gospel from bad Christians. Therefore, whatever happens to us or the Gospel, let us honour our leaders, love them and have faith that they do a very good job.

10 Experiencing God's Presence

Introduction

An important requirement for Bible teaching is that we Christians should know in our life the presence and power of God. If we learn the teaching and apply it to ourselves, we should have better results in our life. We should be able to stand for the Gospel and against worldly things. This chapter is about the conditions that have to be fulfilled for the genuine application of Bible teaching. What is necessary is the relationship that we have with God and with each other and with our neighbours, which makes us holy. This does not mean saintly or spiritual, but refers to the quality of our worship of God, that makes us belong to God and be worthy. Holiness is the centre of Christianity. Jesus Christ as the Son of God is interested in this holiness; we are called to holiness. The relationship that we have with God and with our neighbours allows us to experience God's presence, glory and power.

Charles Wesley, the 18th-century hymn-writer, describes so beautifully the full Christian response to God's action in Jesus Christ:

And can it be that I should gain
> an interest in the Saviour's blood?
> Died he for me, who caused our pain;
> for me, who us to death pursued?
> Amazing love! How can it be?
> that thou, my God, shouldst die for me?

> 'Tis mystery all! The Immortal dies
> who can explore His strange design?
> In vain the first-born seraph tries
> to sound the depths of love divine.

'Tis mercy all! Let earth adore,
let angel minds inquire no more.

He left His father's throne above -
so free, so infinite His grace –
emptied himself of all but love,
and bled for Adam's helpless race.
'Tis mercy all, immense and free;
for O my God, it found out me!

Defining God

God is the eternal person, the maker and ruler of the world. He is the only Supreme Being and creator of the universe, who loves, cares for and helps everyone. Many things reveal aspects of God's nature, and His relationship with people and with His creation; however, His many names are significant.

The most outstanding thing about God is that He is invisible, and full of justice and mercy. God is well known by what He does and says. He is an eternal person who is perfect in wisdom, love, righteousness and divine power. God is three persons: Father, Son and Holy Spirit.

Experiencing God's presence applies to what we go through in life to acknowledge God. We gain knowledge and skill by doing work or going through something. Experiencing God is very important, because it involves the presence and the power of God influencing our daily lives. We can feel the Holy Spirit with us in our daily life, and know His ability to do everything. The presence of God allows our life to be illumined. We can have great confidence in the presence of God. However, we sometimes create false limits and do not do what will enable us to experience the presence of God. We must do everything possible to maintain our Christian life, and this can only be achieved when we always experience God's presence in our life.

In order to experience God, we must find out what the Bible says.

If we accept with our heart and exercise faith in what the Bible says, we will experience God in our life. We must worship, obey and love God. Experiencing the Lord's presence plays a vital role in Christianity, since it gives us more strength and assurance of His presence, and it lets our faith grow. Also, it prepares us for the Gospel race and our Christian race too. However, we will not be able to fulfil our calling unless we pay our vows to God and work for the new life we have received. The vow is our promise to God that we will turn away from the bad, vain things we did before accepting Christ as our personal Saviour, and do good things. We must keep and fulfil this vow to God and put on good things.

We were born in sin through Adam and Eve's disobedience to God, when they set their own standards of living. As a result, we are likely to commit sin before we come to Christ. God creates us again: melts moulds and fills our life with His love, power and His blessings, so that we experience the joy of salvation. God changes our old life and puts new life into us, to open the way for us to do good things. This is a spiritual process. However, it is demonstrated publicly for others to bear witness of the presence of God in us. How can they know all about our new life? Here are some proofs: we will have love and care for others, and we always put on good things, to indicate that we have changed from the bad things we did before he came to Christ.

The acceptance of Christ is a contract between God and us, meaning that we have an agreement to do certain things. Both parties have to fulfil the conditions of the contract. We believe that God always does His part, so it is up to us to do what we promise as followers of Christ. We must open a way for God to fill our life with His love, power and blessings, so that we can experience the joy of salvation. Truly, for God to fill our life does not occur overnight, but gradually. Also, it depends on our obedience in doing God's work to fulfil our side of the contract. Since it is a contract, any failure to do the work of God will have results. We may be in the Kingdom of God for our whole life and nothing will happen to us; we are still the same as we were before coming to Christ. We may be seen as

Christians, but inwardly are not, since our life is not filled with God's life. This is why most of us face problems and all sorts of woes in the body of Christ. Some of us even backslide, because we do not experience the presence of God in our lives. Those of us who are still in the Kingdom also lack God's power to heal people and save people's lives.

Ways of Experiencing God's Presence

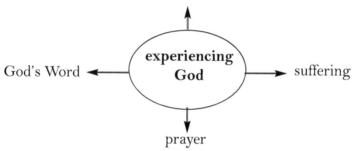

10.1: Experiencing God

Figure 10.1 demonstrates how we can know the presence of God and His power to enable us to accomplish our vision. It shows us the marvellous work of God, so that we can adapt to any situation. We need to know that it is only God who knows the things of tomorrow, what may happen in our life and how we can fulfil our vision. God is always concerned about His children living in the world at a time of violence and malpractice. There is a real danger that keeping distant from Him will certainly give extreme advantage to enemies like Satan. Therefore, He is concerned about the effects of this violence and malpractice in our life.

The system above shows ways for us to experience God, and encourages us to stand firm against problems and temptation. For example, at times we undergo disappointment and failure, before experiencing success or breakthrough, no matter what our relationship with God at that particular moment. It may even be that without disappointment and failure, we will not have success in life.

However, in many cases, experience is the name each one of us gives to our mistakes. We do not recognise that the God who created us is always with us, and therefore will never let us down. God knows that His people will experience joy, pain and sorrow. Therefore, He is with us always to provide, protect and support us. The only thing God needs in return from us is to worship, obey and love Him.

There are many ways for us to experience the presence and power of the Lord's love and care so that His vision can be achieved.

God's Word

We can experience God through the Gospel, which is His Word. This can be done by evaluating and examining it; this will help us find out the kind of God we worship. We need to look at the Word of God carefully, to get a deep understanding of it; only this will enable us to apply it constantly to our life. We will know the facts and importance of the Gospel, and so avoid any misunderstanding.

Fellowship with Christians

Fellowship is sharing, participation and partnership with one another. Fellowship with Christians means that all Christians are family. It demonstrates the love of God and lets us understand the importance of the Gospel, and the people of God. This contributes greatly to our experience of God. We can learn from each other and focus on the Gospel. This encourages us to do the work of God, rather than doing other things that allow us to sin. It opens a way for us share our Gospel experience with others, and encourages us to concentrate on the work of God, since encouragement is a very important aspect of our human life, opening a way to success. It will help us to walk in truth, which can enable us to experience God.

Suffering

Suffering is the enduring of trouble or pain. This suffering may be emotional, mental or physical. It always has two main aspects, remote and immediate. The remote aspect is the main root of the suffering or problem. The immediate aspect is its outcome. God, humans and Satan can cause suffering; however, the main ones are humans and Satan.

There are many sorts of suffering in life: *illness, insults, distress and poverty*; all could lead to death. In Christianity, we have to experience these kinds of suffering, since it is through suffering that we can learn more about the Gospel, God's love, His power and help for us to develop both physically and spiritually.

Some suffering comes from God. As we know, many of us blame our friends, parents or families, but some suffering does not come from them at all, but from the Lord Himself. However, suffering is not part of the Lord's purpose for humankind and He has made provision to end all kinds of suffering. We must be aware that the blessings of the Gospel are conditional: we must fulfil the Gospel requirements to be entitled to these blessings. The worship of God is generally based on obedience, in order for us to enjoy life fully. If we experience suffering, it may be caused by God, to open a better way for us. On the other hand, it maybe a punishment for us, to turn away from sin and turn to God. Some suffering is also permitted by God, to find out whether we have faith in Him, or if we can stand in a crisis.

We ourselves can also cause some suffering. We are to blame for much suffering, rather than blaming other people or Satan. Human attitudes and actions always influence us. If we commit a crime or put on habits that we know can be harmful to our health, our life or that of others, this can cause suffering.

Most of the suffering for which we blame people comes from Satan. The Bible states that every human being was born in sin. So, everyone on this earth must experience suffering which is the fruit of this sin. Truly, suffering is experienced day in and day out. It was Adam and Eve who caused it, through their disobedience to God the Creator. This disobedience occurred through Satan's influence when Adam and Eve turned away from God and set their own standards of good and bad. Since then, their disobedience has become a sinful inheritance for all humankind.

We may experience the suffering of failure as well as disappointment, before succeeding in anything. By suffering such things, we are encouraged to be more determined Christians and to put our trust only in God. We must suffer in our life or in our doings before any breakthrough; however, the Lord is there and knows everything even before it happens.

Limits to Experiencing God's Presence

Limits to experiencing God's presence means things that stop us experiencing the presence and power of God. The essential requirement for experiencing God is the application of God's Word. Knowing God and His Word are the keys that open all the hidden treasures of God's wisdom and knowledge. To know God is to get rid of all the sins in our past life that God has forgiven us, and to keep away from sin in the new life.

What is Sin?

Sin is the breaking of the law of God on purpose, because of something we have in mind to obtain or do. This includes wrongdoings such as *stealing, lying, cheating, destroying marriage, insults, hateful feelings and backbiting*, especially for fame or position. Some of us plan something evil against someone; others of us lie to win our case and carry out plans to hurt others.

God has a purpose for each and every one of us. The Lord's purpose for us is to have control and power over all creatures on the earth. Sin is the key weapon that Satan uses to take someone from the hands of God. Satan knows that when we sin, we break the laws of God on purpose, and therefore God has no control over us, so there is no God to hear or save us when we call to God for help. This is because our sin has separated us from God; the Holy Spirit has no more control of our life. God will not use His power to rescue us from the hands of Satan unless we confess our sin. The main purpose of Satan is to let us endure suffering, pain and destruction. During the period of sin, Satan will try as much as he can to make sure we continue sinning, and to expand our work in order to fulfil our mission. Satan is aware that our work is not going to do us any good, but he will adopt strategies to make us continue to sin. Our sins separate us from God even when we try to worship God.

Sin is the main factor needs to be controlled in everyday life. Getting rid of sin and keeping away from it opens a way to experience God. The human body, referred to as the flesh, is the main cause of this sin, so it must be controlled. Controlling sin is keeping away from things that are contrary to the Gospel, so that there may be no contamination in the body to influence our life and the Gospel. Unfortunately, we are very interested in God's grace, but we continue to live in sin so that the grace of God will increase.

Sin can mean fighting for personal things and destroying people's lives. This is one of our biggest problems. Unfortunately, we are willing to keep doing this, since we believe that, if we have been baptised, all our sins are forgiven and God will continue to forgive us. We even think that if we sin, all we need to do is fast and pray, and then God will forgive us. Therefore, we do not mind about doing bad things to our neighbours.

The main cause of our instability is a lack of deep understanding of the Gospel, faith and the Christian ability to do things. We do not know that it is the Holy Spirit that brings us knowledge of Christ, which is the Bread of Life, food for both our physical and spiritual lives. However, we do not have this knowledge of Christ so we are incapable in our daily life. Many of us are enslaved because of the worthless deceit of human wisdom. Some people cheat us with their knowledge and empty deceit, based on the basic principles of the world. These do not come from Jesus Christ, since these people use human wisdom and teachings, which do not benefit but rather destroy us.

All this impossible wisdom deceives and prevents us being filled with courage and true Gospel teachings, being drawn together in love with true understanding and the full wealth of assurance. We have no knowledge that what we hear or read in the Bible has to be applied in our life. We take the worship of God as a fashion that cheats us. The Gospel and the worship of God are now a means by which we achieve our personal aims. We think that the aim of worship is to show off our personality and our personal things, without realising that these are things of the world that have nothing to do with the Gospel of Christ.

We all have the ability to sin and do whatever we wish. However, we should know that we are allowed to do anything, but that not everything is good for us, so we are not going to let anything make us slaves. God always looks at our desires, since He gives each and every one of us an opportunity to do anything. However, the desire and end of humankind are the concern of God, and so are more important than anything else.

One thing we should know is that Christianity is not about do and don't. It is about following Jesus Christ and His Word, which is practical. It is surprising that many of us go to church to see signs, to look for worldly things or a type of food that spoils or damages life, instead of going to church for the food that can give life.

To get rid of sin in our everyday life means taking spiritual things seriously; this requires love, determination and hard work. Doing spiritual things contributes greatly to our physical and spiritual lives, since we will be able to experience God's presence and power through the Holy Spirit, enabling us to fulfil our mission.

Outcomes of Sin

The outcomes of sin are the things that happen if we commit sin. Sin comes from not doing God's work. Hearing or reading the teachings of the Gospel and not doing what it says is the main problem that leads us to sin. God is always looking for us to apply the Gospel in our lives, since this can help us turn away from sin. Doing what the Gospel says means that we listen to God and want to be saved, and God will make it happen.

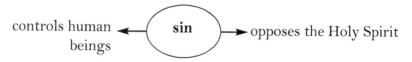

controls human beings ← sin → opposes the Holy Spirit

10.2: Outcomes of sin

Sin causes a bad relationship in our new life. It separates us from the Holy Spirit and makes us discouraged and unhappy. Separation from the Holy Spirit means that we do not have the authority to fight against anything bad. Thus, our situation is at risk, as a result of the aim of Satan to use us. Satan hopes that we will go back and put on earthly desires, and not get rid of them. The consequential change in the outcome of our Gospel work is very serious and dangerous, because the Holy Spirit protects us from danger. This change makes a terrible difference to our physical and spiritual life. A further change occurs if we wholeheartedly seek God's forgiveness and are willing to reject that sin. Our separation from the Holy Spirit is very risky, since it does not do us any good and allows our life to be dominated by evil desires.

Controls human beings

This is the power of sin over the people of God. If we sin, we will be destroyed by our own sins and suffer miserably. Sin comes from Satan, who knows all these things; however, he convinces us to sin, in order to destroy us. Satan also understands that it is by the means of sin that he can take us from the hands of God. Therefore, he is always updating and implementing his strategies, so that we will fall into sin. His aim is to make sure that we will never be saved; he wants us to suffer and endure pain, and wants to destroy us, both physically and spiritually.

One thing about Satan is that he allows us our own free will, as God does. The difference is protection and prevention. God loves and cares for us, protects and prevents us from doing wrong things, while Satan encourages us to sin in order to get us and destroy us. Satan knows that if we respect God's Word, trust in Him, and follow His teachings, our life will be full of joy and gladness. This is because the law of God brings us light, it saves us and leads us to victory all the time. Knowing this, Satan does not want it to happen; therefore, he always tries as much as possible to stop us. He does this by influencing us one way or other to disregard the Word of God, to follow our own wishes, which lead to sin. He knows that our sin will separate us from God, even if we try to worship God. There is nothing good or attractive about the work of Satan that can benefit us. However, our attention is always drawn to Satan's work, because we think that this leads to success.

We must know that sin will do us no good, so we should turn away from it and keep our life holy.

Opposes the Holy Spirit

This refers to being against the work of the Holy Spirit. An important power of the Holy Spirit is that He controls us, and helps us achieve the Gospel mission. The Holy Spirit has authority to use us, both in our physical and spiritual daily life, so that we do not reject the commands of God to turn away from what God shows us is right.

However, we do not listen to God, and we rebel against God as result of sin. We oppose the Lord's plans through sin, and let ourselves be controlled by the power of the world's spiritual rulers and authorities. Such opposition makes us belong to the world and keep our minds fixed on worldly things. When we sin, we break the law of God. Once the law is broken, it draws the Holy Spirit away from us, and we become empty: there is no power and control from the Holy Spirit. The Holy Spirit is holy, so anything we do against the Word of God will automatically take us away from Him. If this happens, it allows Satan to have control over us. The Holy Spirit who guards us is not able to function as previously. There is nothing that God cannot do because He has authority over all things; however, since God is holy and has given each one of us our own will, He is not in a position to assist us sinners.

Then there will be a time of trouble caused by Satan. When this time occurs, things will turn out differently and our motives will be evil, until we turn to God for forgiveness. God does not want us to be punished, but our wishes will bring trouble upon us. It may seem that God is ignoring us. That is not the case since God is great and He honours everyone. He is faithful to His covenant, and shows constant love to His people who love Him and do what His Word says.

If our situation changes from doing wrong to doing right, this allows the Holy Spirit to take control and close the gap between us and the Holy Spirit. This change is a biblical result of us doing the right thing. Then the Holy Spirit monitors us to achieve the Gospel goals. However, if the situation does not change and we remain in wrongdoing, it causes terrible destruction and we will be unsuccessful in everything. This will be the case, even if it looks good and successful at the beginning. Therefore, if we sin, we oppose the plans of God. We will be controlled by the power of the world's spiritual rulers and authorities instead of the Holy Spirit, and we will be led to an unsuccessful end and destruction.

In fact, we need to understand that Satan is still active. He is capable of launching an attack on us, especially on believers, to destroy our lives. Jesus came and died on the cross to save our lives. So we should be very careful not to be led by our feelings and assumptions, but by the Holy Spirit to achieve our ambition.

Our main work is the work of God, to love and take care of the Gospel and needy people. How can we do this? Can we do it with all the malpractice going on in the body of Christ? This is definitely impossible. It can only be achieved by combating false Christians and organised crime in the church of Christ, in order to continue to maintain the safety of the church and public confidence in the Gospel.

Moreover, we must always show our deepest love and care to the public, especially at the most painful times, like Christmas and times of war around the world. At times like Christmas, people are lonely, feeling that they have nobody to listen to them, or feeling that they have been rejected. In times of war, people lose parents or families, or lose all their belongings. These are the most significant times when we can demonstrate the love of Jesus Christ to His people.

Doing this will let others know the kind of God we worship, and the main role of the believers in the Gospel. It will also encourage people to understand that the God of Abraham, Isaac and Jacob loves them and cares for them, no matter what they are, since they are His children. This will provide assurance of Christ's love and care and His final victory, to make their lives better and allow them to decide to come into the body of Christ.

In fact, if we call ourselves genuine followers of Christ, there must be a campaign to put pressure on the body of Christ, to provide protection for all believers of Christ; for instance, those who indirectly force us to contribute to the body of Christ beyond our abilities and wishes, since this damages the Gospel, people's lives and the public at large.

Oh Lord! do not let money or the things of this world become part of us, since they have nothing to do with the Gospel. Let Your love and care for people be the main roots of Your church. Help us to see and deeply understand Your Gospel and resurrection. Open our minds and our hearts to believe in and accept Your Son Jesus Christ of Bethlehem and Nazareth. Let us work with Christ with open hearts, to focus and concentrate on Him only, rather than on the world.

Our dear Lord, remind Your children day in and day out, so that we may realise that there is life after death, and that therefore we should not worry about the things of this world or depend on human beings. Remind us to focus on You, the Lord, the Maker of everything, and worship You sincerely, since you have promised us Your everlasting blessings and that You will never fail us.

We have to concentrate on Jesus Christ by applying His teachings. We must trust in the Lord with all our hearts and not depend on our own understanding, will or the world. Also, we must have humility and fear of the Lord, because this will help our spiritual growth and bring us wealth, honour and life. It will enable us to study our Lord's ways and lead us in a straight path.

If we want to be true disciples and great people of God, we have to take responsibility for other people, based on love and care, as the Good Samaritan did. This can only be achieved by preparing, reminding and renewing ourselves for Christ's Second Coming and by fellowship with one another, rather than by following the world. It is not easy to have fellowship with one another in this world. Jesus Christ, who sits at the right hand of God and deals with our circumstances and enemies, will make our circumstances much better and make our enemies a footstool for our feet. He will help us rule especially in the midst of our enemies, and achieve our ambitions and expectations, which are the second coming of Christ.

We have to look to Jesus and not to people. Our character or attitude should be the same as that of Jesus Christ to become 'nothing' as the Lord Himself became 'nothing' on the cross for us. We have to become disciples of loss, instead of disciples of gain; we should serve, sacrifice and set aside all selfish attitudes and personal ambitions. Some of us are sometimes not sad to hear that our brothers and sisters in Christ are in difficulty or that they face problems. We must free ourselves from burdens such as fighting for financial, property, position and domineering attitudes in the Kingdom of God, in order to fulfil our Father's desire for us.

The Lord descended from the perfection of Heaven to the imperfection of earth and to the cross, to save all of us. He came from the unlimited God to the limited body of a human, and from sinless to sin-stained, because of our sin. The one who possesses everything became nothing. He did not use His power and position to manipulate or condemn people. Who are we to use our position and achievements to treat our brothers and sisters badly, as well as to criticise and use the name of the Lord to cheat and steal from people? Most of our lives have to be changed, because we desperately wish to experience the power and the glory of our Lord; otherwise, nothing good will happen to our lives. This is simply because our attitudes and behaviour evidently deny the Lord; we constantly pollute the Gospel of Christ without even thinking of refraining from our sin. Still, we intentionally and persistently declare ourselves to be true followers of Christ, whilst inwardly we are not. The church has to focus on continuing improvement, to ensure that we develop to our full potential, enabling us to reach people outside with the good news, for the benefit of the public and the Gospel.

May the God of Abraham, Isaac and Jacob help us to refrain from chasing the things of the world, and to worship Him intimately. Also, may He help us know our position in Him, open our eyes and give us understanding, like King Solomon, with wisdom and knowledge to worship Him sincerely and permanently. This will enable us to grow and develop, to fulfil His vision for us and glorify His Name.

Again, it is my prayer that the Maker of heaven and earth will redeem us once again and renew our hearts. May He let the angels help us to worship, serve and adore Him sincerely, and help us play our role in the Gospel, to enable the Children of God to fulfil God's plans and will.

May He bless you all.
Amen!

Lightning Source UK Ltd.
Milton Keynes UK
UKHW02f0433240618
324686UK00003BA/81/P